Rebecca Geoghegan
Jill Carter

Introduction

How this workbook will help you

This workbook aims to provide you with an accessible introduction to the basics of spelling, punctuation and grammar. The workbook focuses on what you need to know to write fluently and accurately through supportive teaching text and a range of targeted activities.

How this workbook is structured

The workbook is split into three chapters, covering spelling, punctuation and grammar. Each topic in the chapters includes key teaching information and explanation, followed by a range of structured activities to test your understanding.

The workbook also has a clear focus on spelling, punctuation and grammar in context. Selected topics across the workbook feature an 'in context' spread; these spreads include a carefully-selected source text extract and a range of activities that ask you to consider how and why the author has used a particular technique for effect.

Exploring new texts

This workbook introduces you to a range of fiction and non-fiction texts from different historical periods (from the 19th, 20th and 21st centuries), which will help to prepare you for the type of texts you will encounter throughout your English studies.

Which features are included?

The workbook offers a range of varied activities to test your understanding of all the spelling, punctuation and grammar topics, as well as tasks that challenge you to explore the effects of specific grammatical choices in source text extracts. There are spaces to write your answers throughout.

Throughout this workbook, you will find 'Key terms' and 'Tips' to help support your understanding of difficult concepts, along with a 'Find out more' feature that will direct you to other related topics in the workbook.

For ease of reference, there is also a complete glossary at the end of the workbook that explains all of the relevant spelling, punctuation and grammar terms used throughout the book.

1 Nouns

What are nouns?

A noun names a person, place, feeling, idea or thing.

How do they work?

Nouns can be divided into different groups as follows:

Common nouns

A common noun names general things rather than specific ones.

teacher	street	candle

Proper nouns

A proper noun names a specific person, place or thing. It always begins with a **capital letter**.

Neill Street	Peru	Jim

Concrete nouns

A concrete noun names something that can be touched, smelled, tasted, heard or seen.

wood	music	coffee

Abstract nouns

An abstract noun names a concept, feeling or idea.

greed	hate	marriage

A good way to identify a noun is to try adding the word 'the' in front of it.

Key term

capital letter an upper case letter, e.g. A, B or C.

See pages 48–51 for more about Capital Letters

A concrete noun names something that can be **touched**, **smelled**, **tasted**, **heard** or **seen**.

Activity 1

Decide whether the noun in bold is a common or proper noun and circle the correct letter. The first one has been done for you.

a) It was **(a / Ⓐ)melia's** dream to be a professional diver.

b) Our class heard **(m / M)r (s / S)mith** shouting at a boy in the hallway!

c) My trip to planet **(z / Z)appo** is booked for next year.

d) Diego's **(t / T)eacher** was angry that he was late.

e) The **(d / D)octor** wrote her prescription.

f) Chelsea beat Crystal **(p / P)alace** on Saturday.

/6

Activity 2

Decide whether each of the nouns below is common or proper and concrete or abstract.

Noun	Common or proper?	Concrete or abstract?
curry	common	concrete
guitar		
friendship		
trees		
religion		
lemonade		
William		
money		

/14

Activity 3

Write three proper nouns that belong in the common noun group listed in the first column. The first two have been completed for you.

Common noun	Proper noun 1	Proper noun 2	Proper noun 3
country	France	Croatia	
sports brands			
TV shows			
names			

/10

Tip

Remember, every word of a proper noun starts with a capital letter, e.g. Blackstock School. In this example, 'School' needs a capital too because it is part of the proper noun.

2 Pronouns

What are pronouns?

Pronouns can take the place of a noun. They are used to avoid repeating a noun or **noun phrase**.

For example, 'Sam paid for the drink. Then Sam took the change' could be confusing as it suggests that there might be more than one person called Sam.

'Sam paid for the drink. Then he took the change' makes it clear that one person called Sam paid for the drink and took the change.

How do they work?

Personal pronouns

Personal pronouns are used in place of a noun that refers to a person, people or a thing. Personal pronouns can replace either the **subject** or the **object** of a verb in a sentence.

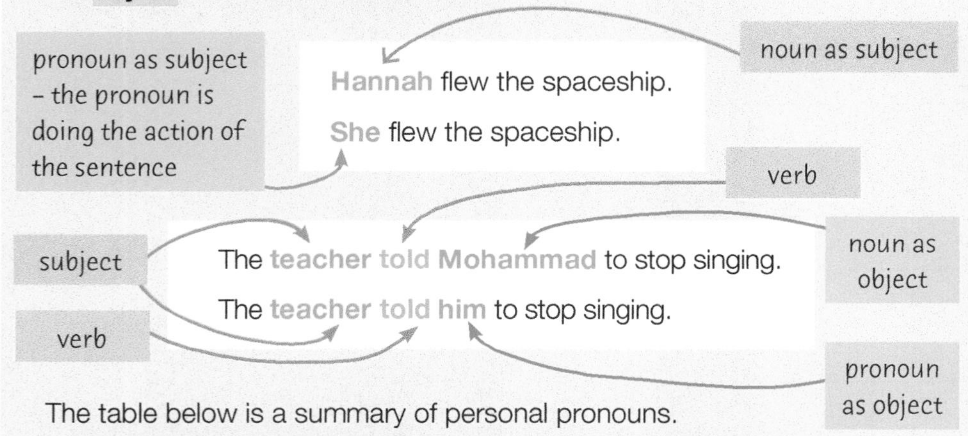

The table below is a summary of personal pronouns.

	Singular	Plural
First person	Subject: I Object: me	Subject: we Object: us
Second person	Subject: you Object: you	Subject: you Object: you
Third person	Subject: he, she, it Object: him, her, it	Subject: they Object: them

Key terms

noun phrase a group of words that acts as a noun and has a noun as its headword

object the object in a sentence is the person, animal or thing that is on the receiving end of the action (having something done to it)

subject the person, animal or thing in a sentence that is doing or being the verb

Tip

When referring to yourself and other people check that you are using the correct form of the first-person pronoun by removing the other people from the sentence. If it still makes sense, then you've used the correct form, e.g. 'Misha and me went to the cinema.' If you take 'Misha' out of the sentence, it doesn't make sense. You wouldn't say 'Me went to the cinema.' It should be 'Misha and I went to the cinema.'

Activity 1

Tick the sentences where the personal pronoun has been used correctly.

Her ate dinner in front of the TV.	
She gave them pancakes for breakfast.	
It lives in a cage in the garage.	
Me called the number that Joe wrote down.	
At the skate park them met up with the others.	
The cloud rained on her just as she shut the front door.	
Flynn's mother took him to the karate lesson on Saturday.	
Every day they walk past the blue house.	

/8

Activity 2

Circle the subject pronouns and underline the object pronouns in the following paragraph.

Bryony knew that she had to face up to it and tackle the climbing wall in front of her. Josie and Sara had already managed the challenge and they seemed to have coped just fine with it. She knew she could do it; she could definitely do it. The wall was high but it had enough footholds and it was certainly no more of a challenge than the white-water rafting had been. Josie and Sara might be good climbers but so was she!

/13

Activity 3

Tick the three sentences which use personal pronouns incorrectly and rewrite them correctly underneath.

I suggested Marnie Lauder as a candidate but her withdrew from the election.	
The banana is quite cheap and it's definitely a healthy food.	
Us three all love chips.	
Having bought the trousers, I realised they didn't suit me.	
Samir and me are coming to the party.	
The world is made up of rich and poor; it is not an equal place.	

/6

Possessive pronouns

A possessive pronoun refers to something that is owned. Possessive pronouns are **mine**, **hers**, **his**, **yours**, **its**, **ours** and **theirs**.

The job you applied for is yours!   That football is hers.

A possessive pronoun does not come before a noun. It stands in place of a noun.

Relative pronouns

A relative pronoun refers one part of a sentence to another. Relative pronouns are:

who, **whom**, **whose** – if you are referring to people

which, **that** – if you are referring to things.

Use 'who' if the pronoun is replacing a noun that is the subject of the verb. Use 'whom' if the pronoun is replacing the object of the verb.

relative pronoun referring to a person, the man

This is the book that Darwin wrote.

Alexander Graham Bell was the man who invented the telephone.

relative pronoun referring to a thing, the book

Use 'that' to introduce a **clause** that is essential to the sense of the sentence.

Use 'which' to introduce a clause that is not essential to the overall sense of the sentence.

This clause is needed to make sense of the first clause in the sentence.

This clause could be removed from the sentence and it would still make sense.

It is the same moped that Enzo's dad has.

She caught the spaceship, which was late as usual, to go to Mars.

Key term

clause a group of words that work together as a unit with a verb as its headword

She caught the spaceship, **which was late as usual**, to go to Mars.

Activity 4

Sort the following list into the boxes.

his mine hers her yours ours its theirs

me I she he you it them us we

Personal pronouns	Possessive pronouns

/17

Activity 5

Add the correct relative pronoun to each sentence.

a) David caught the girl _______ had just fainted in the queue to meet the band.

b) The harness, ___________ was attached to the rope above her, was the only thing stopping her from falling to the bottom of the cliff.

c) My team mate, __________ older sister dropped us at training, had forgotten her kit so had to play in her school uniform.

d) We really enjoyed the film ___________ we saw last night.

e) He missed the song, __________ was his favourite, as the couple on the next table drowned it out with their arguing.

f) So this is the new dance teacher about ___________ I have heard so much.

/6

Activity 6

Circle the relative pronouns in the following paragraph.

The dog, which was always escaping its owner, hurtled down the street towards the skateboarder who was looking the other way. This was an accident that could be avoided, Robbie thought to himself. He plunged towards the skateboarder and pushed him off his board onto the grass which at least made for a soft landing. The dog bundled on top of both of them and the man the dog belonged to arrived a few minutes later, apologising profusely.

Add two more sentences that include a relative pronoun to this paragraph.

/6

Tip

In a more formal text, you could write 'the man to whom the dog belonged'.

Nouns and pronouns in context

Extract from *The Condition of the Working Class in England* by Friedrich Engels

This book was written during Friedrich Engels' stay in Manchester from 1842 to 1844 and first published in English in 1887. Here, he describes the life of a family living in a slum.

On Monday, Jan. 15th, 1844, two boys were brought before the police **magistrate** because, being in a starving condition, they had stolen and immediately devoured a half-cooked calf's foot from a shop. The magistrate felt called upon to investigate the case further, and received the following details from the policeman: The mother
5 of the two boys was the widow of an ex-soldier, afterwards policeman, and had had a very hard time since the death of her husband, to provide for her nine children. She lived at No. 2 Pool's Place, Quaker Court, Spitalfields, in the utmost poverty. When the policeman came to her, he found her with six of her children literally huddled together in a little back room, with no furniture but two old rush-bottomed chairs with the
10 seats gone, a small table with two legs broken, a broken cup, and a small dish. On the hearth was scarcely a spark of fire, and in one corner lay as many old rags as would fill a woman's apron, which served the whole family as a bed. For bed clothing they had only their **scanty** day clothing. The poor woman told him that she had been forced to sell her bedstead the year before to buy food. Her bedding she had **pawned** with the
15 **victualler** for food. In short, everything had gone for food.

magistrate judge
scanty inadequate, small in quantity
pawned left with a pawnbroker as security for money lent
victualler food and drink seller

Activity 1 Understanding the text

a) What have the two boys been brought before the magistrate for?

---

b) Why did they do it?

---

c) How many children does the mother have?

---

d) What two jobs did her late husband have?

e) What did she hand over to the victualler?

Activity 2 Exploring the writer's technique

a) Why does every word in the phrase 'No. 2 Pool's Place, Quaker Court, Spitalfields' start with a capital letter?

b) Circle the nouns in the following sentence. What is the effect of the long list of nouns?

'… he found her with six of her children literally huddled together in a little back room, with no furniture but two old rush-bottomed chairs with the seats gone, a small table with two legs broken, a broken cup, and a small dish.'

c) The writer does not use the pronouns 'I' or 'me' in the extract. Write a sentence explaining why you think Engels chooses not to do this.

Activity 3 Try it yourself

On a separate piece of paper, write a police statement imagining that you have been robbed.

Include details of who, what, when and where. Use nouns and pronouns to make your statement specific and clear.

3 Adjectives

What are adjectives?

An adjective describes a noun or pronoun. Adjectives are used to give information or to modify nouns or pronouns.

> She stuffed her **faded** jeans and **checked** shirt into her **battered** suitcase.

How do they work?

Descriptive adjectives

A descriptive adjective describes the quality of a noun or pronoun.

> The **secretive** man.

Adjectives can also follow the verb 'to be' and are used to describe the noun that is the subject of the verb.

> The man is **secretive**.

Possessive adjectives

Possessive adjectives, or possessive **determiners**, show ownership of a noun. Possessive adjectives include her, his, my, your, our, its and their.

> **My** phone vibrated.

Comparative adjectives

A comparative adjective compares one noun or pronoun with another. Add the **suffix –er** to the adjective or add the word more followed by than.

> Jamie was **taller** than Matt.

Superlative adjectives

A superlative adjective compares three or more nouns or pronouns. Add the before the adjective, then add the suffix –est to the adjective or add the word most.

> It was the **biggest** pumpkin I have ever seen!

Key terms

determiner a word that comes before a noun and gives more information about it, such as which one it is, how many there are, where it is and whose it is, e.g. an, that or some

suffix a letter or letters added to the end of a root word to form another word, e.g. **–er** added to 'tall' creates the word 'taller'

See pages 79–80 for more about suffixes.

She stuffed her **faded** jeans and **checked** shirt into her **battered** suitcase.

Activity 1

The adjectives in the sentences below have been highlighted in bold. For each sentence, write down whether the adjective is: descriptive, possessive, comparative or superlative.

a) **My** iguana loves me. ____________

b) The princess's polished **golden** crown is missing. ____________

c) I hate to admit that she is **funnier** than me. ____________

d) The **damp** smell of the prison made him feel homesick. ____________

e) **Our** team tracked down the culprit. ____________

f) David was the **youngest** brother. ____________

g) **Her** bedroom window reflected the moonlight. ____________

h) Daisy was **quieter** than a mouse. ____________

i) It gave me the **greatest** pleasure to see her smile. ____________

/9

Activity 2

Underline the correct choice of comparative or superlative adjectives in the following sentences.

a) The party was the (best/bestest) that Tariq had ever been to.

b) Sofia was (happiest/happier) than Imogen.

c) Massimo's cherry cupcake was (larger/largest) than hers.

d) He was pleased that his bike was (cooler/coolest) than anyone else's.

e) Amy used the (softest/softer) wool to knit the baby's blanket.

f) I settled down to read the (latest/later) update from the director.

/6

Activity 3

Add descriptive adjectives to this description of a fairground.

On the edge of the ____________ town, the ____________ fairground had set up its ____________ rides for the locals to enjoy. Each night for a week, ____________ lights filled the ____________ sky, and the ____________ sound of music could be heard: calling the ____________ people to enjoy its ____________ delights. As they got closer, they could smell the ____________ food ready to fill their ____________ stomachs. ____________ children squealed delightedly at the sight of the rides, trying to convince their ____________ parents to pay for them to have a go.

/12

Tip

Use a thesaurus to improve your descriptive adjectives and keep a record of those more unusual ones for another time.

Adjectives in context

Extract from *Great Expectations* by Charles Dickens

The novel *Great Expectations* was published in 1861. It tells the story of Pip and his journey from boyhood to adulthood. Here he first enters the room of the bitter spinster, Miss Havisham.

I crossed the staircase landing, and entered the room she indicated. From that room, too, the daylight was completely excluded, and it had an airless smell that was **oppressive**. A fire had been lately kindled in the damp, old-fashioned grate, and it was more disposed to go out than to burn up, and the reluctant smoke which
5 hung in the room seemed colder than the clearer air – like our own marsh mist. Certain wintry branches of candles in the high chimney-piece faintly lighted the **chamber**; or, it would be more expressive to say, faintly troubled its darkness. It was spacious, and I dare say had once been handsome, but every **discernible** thing in it was covered with dust and mould, and dropping to pieces. The most prominent
10 object was the long table with a tablecloth spread on it, as if a feast had been in preparation when the house and the clocks stopped together. An epergne or centre-piece of some kind was in the middle of this cloth; it was quite **indistinguishable**; and, as I looked along the yellow expanse out of which I remember its seeming to grow, like a black fungus, I saw speckle-legged spiders with blotchy bodies running
15 home to it, and running out from it, as if some circumstance of the greatest public importance had just **transpired** in the spider community.

oppressive heavy and harsh
chamber room
discernible visible
indistinguishable unclear, unidentifiable
transpired happened

Activity 1 Understanding the text

a) What is Pip doing in the extract?

---

b) What has been lit?

---

c) What is 'the most prominent object' in the room?

---

d) What are living in the centrepiece?

Activity 2 Exploring the writer's technique

a) What atmosphere do the descriptive adjectives 'airless' and 'oppressive' create?

b) Why has the writer used the comparative adjectives 'colder than the clearer air'?

c) In an essay, a student wrote:

'The use of the superlative adjective "most prominent" in the phrase "The most prominent object was the long table" is so our attention is drawn away from everything else to the table.'

Explain why you agree or disagree with this statement.

d) What atmosphere is created by the descriptive adjectives 'black' and 'yellow'?

Activity 3 Try it yourself

Look at this photo and write a short paragraph describing the scene. Think carefully about your use of the different types of adjectives.

4 Verbs

What are verbs?

A verb is often referred to as a 'doing word'. It describes an action or a state of being. There is always a verb in every sentence or clause.

How do they work?

Action verbs

Action verbs describe physical actions.

Mario **danced** the night away.   The cat **sat** on my head.

State verbs

State verbs describe mental actions, states of being or possession.

I **hate** sprouts.   Emily **wants** new trainers.

Auxiliary verbs

An auxiliary verb helps the main verb make sense in a sentence. It can be used to give information about the mood and **tense.** Tense tells us when an action is carried out.

Be (including **is**, **are**, **am**, **was** and **were**), **do** (including **does** and **did**) and **have** (including **has** and **had**) are all auxiliary verbs.

She **washes** the dog. (main verb)

She **is washing** the dog. (auxiliary verb explains tense; main verb)

Did he **see** the wet paint sign? (auxiliary verb makes a question; main verb)

Modal verbs

A modal verb is a type of auxiliary verb. We use modal verbs to express possibility, necessity or the future.

The modal verbs are **can**, **could**, **may**, **might**, **must**, **shall**, **should**, **w** and **would**. Shall is used with I and we; all other pronouns use will.

Key term

tense the three main verb tenses are past tense, present tense and future; they explain whether something is happening now, has already happened, or will happen in the future

Find out more

See pages 20–23 for more about tenses.

The cat **sat** on my head.

modal verb indicates future

modal verb indicates possibility

You will be late if you don't get up soon!

I might apply for that job.

You ought to tie your laces before you go running.

main verb

main verb

modal verb indicates necessity

main verb

Activity 1

Read the sentences below and write an A (action) or S (state) next to each sentence for the type of verb used.

a) She sings with a local choir. ____________________

b) Asher packed his school bag for the morning. ____________________

c) The cook needs a new mango cheesecake recipe. ________________

d) My cousin loved her parachute jump. ____________________

/4

Activity 2

Add the correct auxiliary verb to the following sentences to put them in the present tense.

a) _______ you know what time we are supposed to be at court?

b) A sheepdog _____ running around the street.

c) _______ we have a Mandarin lesson tomorrow?

d) Dr Phillips' patients ______ waiting very patiently.

/4

Tip

'Of' and 'have' are often confused. Avoid this by remembering that the modal verbs 'could', 'should' and 'would' are always paired with 'have' – 'could have', 'should have', 'would have'.

Activity 3

Using modal verbs, write a sentence giving advice for the problem.

a) I have a toothache.

You should go to the dentist.

b) I have forgotten my front door key.

----

c) I've lost my pet scorpion.

----

d) I smashed my phone screen.

/4

Verbs in context

Extract from *Cloudstreet* by Tim Winton

The novel *Cloudstreet* (published in 1991) is set in Perth, Australia during the 1940s and 50s. Here the young man, Quick Lamb, has rowed out to sea to fish for his family.

About five hundred yards out, over a wide patch of sandy bottom, he dropped the hook and felt the boat hang back on it. He baited up and then it began. The first bite rang in his wrist like the impact of a **cover drive**, a bat and ball jolt in his **sinews**. From below, a skipjack **broadsided** and bore down on the hook in its
5 **palate**, sending water springing from the line as it came up. Then he saw another lunging towards it, and when he hauled the first into the boat, it was two fish, one fixed to the tail of the other. They thumped in the bottom round his ankles, the size of big silver slippers. He baited up again and cast out. He got a strike the moment the hook hit the water, and then another, and when he saw the upwards charge
10 of the mob he felt something was happening that he might not be able to explain to a stranger. He dragged in four fish, two hooked and two biting their tails. He caught them cast after cast, sometimes three to a hook, with one fish fixed to the passenger fish. His hands bled and his arms ached. In his eyes the sweat rolled and boiled. Now the boat vibrated like a cathedral with all these fish arching, beating,
15 sliding, bucking, hammering. In the water they bludgeoned themselves against the timbers, shine running off them in lurches, stirring the deep sandy bottom into a rising cloudbank until Quick was throwing out baitless hooks to drag in great silver chains of them. They shone like money. They slid and slicked about his knees. Quick Lamb's breathing got to be a hacking just short of a cough, and in the end he
20 stopped casting and lay back in the smother and squelch of fish as they leapt into the boat of their own accord.

cover drive a cricket shot
sinews tissue linking muscle and bone
broadsided hit
palate roof of the mouth

Activity 1 Understanding the text

a) What is Quick doing in the opening sentence of the paragraph?

----

b) How far out is Quick when he 'drops the hook'?

----

c) What is the first type of fish that Quick catches?

d) What does Quick do when he gets tired?

Activity 2 Exploring the writer's technique

a) What does the verb 'rang' in line 3 suggest about the effect of the fish on Quick?

b) What is the effect of the modal verb 'might' in the phrase 'he might not be able to explain' (line 10)?

c) What is the effect of the list of verbs 'arching, beating, sliding, bucking, hammering' (lines 14–15) used to describe the actions of the fish?

d) Explain how the writer uses verbs to show the difference in Quick's actions at the beginning and at the end of the extract.

Activity 3 Try it yourself

Imagine you are a travel writer wandering around a new city. Write a paragraph describing the actions happening in this photo. Include interesting details about the actions of each person you see.

Verb tenses: past, present and future

What are tenses?

A tense tells us whether an action or thought has happened (past), is happening (present) or will happen (future).

How do they work?

Past tense

The past tense describes actions that have already happened.

The simple past form of most regular verbs is made by adding the suffix **–ed**.

past participle of 'play' → I played football on Saturday.

Irregular verbs do not follow a pattern when forming the past participle, for example, 'write' becomes 'wrote'.

present tense → He writes a blog post.

past tense → He wrote a blog post.

Some common irregular verbs are:

Present tense (he/she/it)	Past tense
is	was
makes	made
goes	went
does	does
gets	got
knows	knew
taker	took
eats	ate

Key term

irregular verb a verb that changes in a unique way, not following the usual pattern and often changing the root of the word

Find out more

See pages 22–23 for more about the present tense.

I **watched** the football on Saturday.

Activity 1

a) Tick the sentences below that are written in the past tense.

I will always love that ice cream parlour.	
Angel knew that she couldn't eat too much sugar without feeling sick.	
One option was for Rory to leave home.	
Benoit struck the hammer against the lock.	
Natalia lives in the Czech Republic, where she has a lovely family.	

b) Rewrite the sentences that are not in the past tense so that they are written in the past tense.

/7

Activity 2

Rewrite the following sentences in the past tense.

a) She writes in French. --

b) They swim each day in the lake. --

c) The boys ride their bikes to school. --

d) We often meet at the café. --

e) I see him most days. --

f) We sleep in tents in Spain. --

/6

Activity 3

Rewrite the verbs in bold so that the paragraph is in the past tense.

The boat **sails** _________ across the sea towards the island in the distance. It **is** _________ a small island but **is** _________ full of mystery. A light **glows** _________ inside a small building perched on top of the island; the building **looks** _________ like it **is** _________ going to fall into the sea. As the boat **moves** _________ through the water, the waves **swirl** _________ around and **make** _________ for a bumpy journey.

/9

Present tense

The simple present tense describes actions that happen in the present, including habitual actions.

Regular verbs are often used in the **infinitive** form or add the suffix **–s/–es** to form the third-person singular.

We use the present progressive tense to describe actions that are happening now. It is formed using the verb be (am, is or are) as an auxiliary verb plus the present participle of the main verb. The present participle is usually formed by adding **–ing** to the root of the verb.

Future

The future describes actions that have not yet happened and will take place in the future.

The future can be formed by using the infinitive of the main verb plus one of the following:

- the modal verb 'will'
- the modal verb 'shall'.

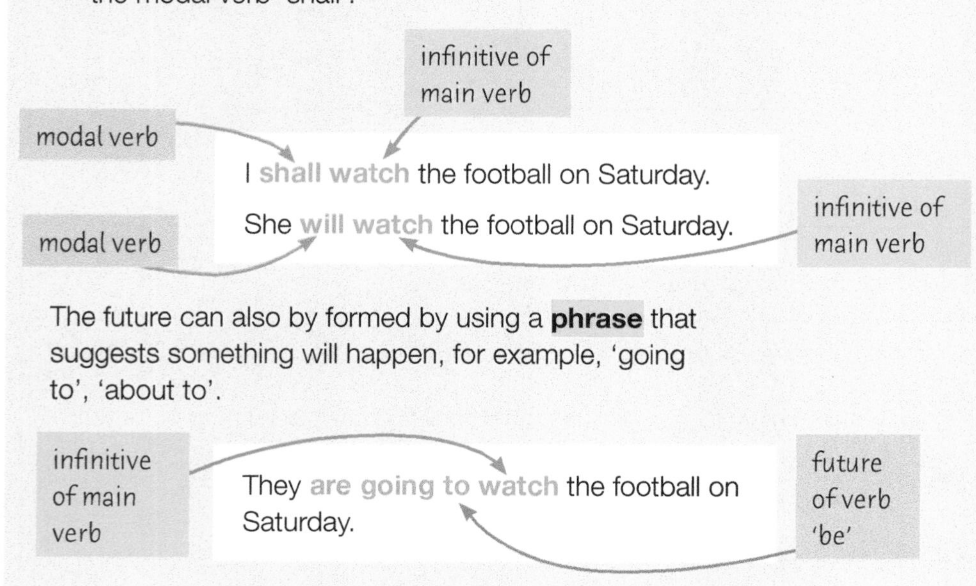

The future can also by formed by using a **phrase** that suggests something will happen, for example, 'going to', 'about to'.

Key terms

infinitive the root, or base form, of a verb. Often has 'to' in front of it, e.g. 'to play'

phrase a group of words that form a unit; most phrases do not have a verb so they are not full sentences

Find out more

See pages 16–17 to find out more about auxiliary and modal verbs.

Activity 4

Underline the correct verb so that the following conversation is in the present tense.

"I am tired," (says/said) Rowen rubbing his eyes.

"Why don't you put your feet up?" Dad (replied/replies).

"I can't, it's my turn to make dinner."

Dad (smiles/smiled). "Let's just get a takeaway."

"We can't," Rowen (exclaims/exclaimed). "We had one last night!"

"It doesn't matter; we can do double time at the gym!"

Rowen (rolled/rolls) his eyes. "OK, I can't be bothered to argue!"

"I knew it!" Dad (exclaimed/exclaims) triumphantly.

/6

Tip

Look for the suffixes (endings) of verbs to work out if it's written in the present, past or future tense.

Activity 5

Rewrite the following paragraph in the present tense a seperate pap.

The world seemed like a huge and frightening place to the boy. Never before had he been lost and alone. The station concourse was vast and his mother was nowhere to be seen. All around him people jostled and shoved for space; their bags and cases were scattered around the floor like impossible obstacles. Suddenly a hand reached out and drew him through a small gap in the crowd and he recognised his mother's desperate shouts. "Raj! Where have you been? Are you OK?"

Write two more sentences in the present tense to complete this paragraph.

/4

Activity 6

Rewrite the following present tense sentences in the future. You could use the verb forms 'am', 'is', 'are', 'going to' or 'will'.

a) I ride my bike.

---

b) Asif and Hannah play basketball on Friday nights.

---

c) The canteen is very full.

---

d) Aliyah's stepmum dropped her off at my house.

/4

6 Active and passive voices

What are the active and passive voices?

The active voice is used when the subject has performed the action in a clause.

The passive voice is used when the subject of the clause has an action done to it by someone or something else. It is used when a writer wants the reader to focus on what happens rather than who does it. However, be careful when using the passive voice: it can make the writing unclear if overused.

Find out more

See pages 6–7 for more about subject and object.

How do they work?

Active voice

This is where the subject of the clause performs the action.

Here 'Ellie' (the subject) is performing the action 'dislike'.

Passive voice

This is where the subject of the clause is acted upon by the verb.

Here 'Marco' becomes the subject. 'Was' is the past tense version of the verb 'be'. 'Disliked' is the action performed upon him. It's useful to practise switching between the active and passive voices.

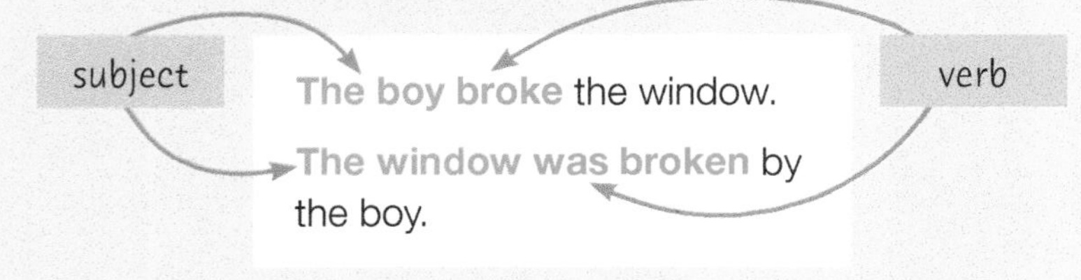

Marco **was disliked** by Ellie.

Activity 1

Write P for passive or A for active for each of the sentences below.

The sleepy boy was woken by his nightmare.	
Marta read the paper on the long submarine journey.	
A river ran through the quiet town nestled in the hills.	
Edward was hit by his guilt during break time.	
The spy waited by the entrance for his contact.	
By lunchtime, the cows had run out of milk.	
Violet was called down to dinner at 6 p.m.	
Huddersfield Youth FC was beaten by Middlesbrough in penalties.	
I stood by the window and watched the shooting star fly through the night sky.	

/9

Activity 2

Rewrite the following sentences to change the active voice into the passive voice.

a) After the accident, the police stopped the traffic until the chickens had been rounded up.

---

b) Later that evening, Mrs Fenn dropped Sam at his ballet class.

---

c) The eager passengers took the early flight out of Rome to Spain.

---

d) My mechanic had to run a diagnostic test on the motorbike engine to see what the problem was.

/4

7 Adverbs

What are adverbs?

Adverbs are used to describe verbs, adjectives, other adverbs or whole sentences. Many adverbs end in **–ly**.

She walked quickly to the end of the queue.

adverb describes how she walked

An adverb phrase has an adverb as its headword and acts in the same way as a single word adverb.

She walked as quickly as she could to the end of the queue.

adverb phrase describes how she walked

An adverbial is an adverb, a phrase or a clause that modifies a verb. Most adverbials are placed at the end of a sentence.

They met yesterday afternoon.

adverbial describing when they met

How do they work?

An adverb can give information about:

- when the action happened (yesterday, later that day)

He went to school yesterday.

- where the action happened (upstairs, outside)

They hunted everywhere for the missing keys.

- how the action happened (happily, quietly)

She sang softly so that no one could hear her.

- how much the action happened (very, quite)

He worked very hard.

Tip

When an adverbial is used at the start of a sentence, it is called a fronted adverbial. They are often used to add emphasis to the action.

Later that day, she called him.

- how often the action happened (frequently, never)

They went swimming every weekend.

- how long the action happened for (all day, all year)

They were on holiday all week.

- opinions on the action (unfortunately, brilliantly).

Fortunately, they remembered their passports.

Activity 1

Add an adverb, adverb phrase or adverbial to the sentences below to add information about *how* the actions happened. Use clues in the sentences to help you with ideas.

a) ________________, his pen stopped working just as the exam started.

b) As the vault door creaked open, a wind blew ________________ through the empty hall.

c) Kate and Laura talked ______________ in case their boss heard them.

d) ________________, she waited for them to call her in for the audition.

e) My front doorbell rang ___________ as I waited for my mysterious visitor to arrive.

/5

Activity 2

The following paragraph includes fronted adverbials, –ly adverbs and adverb phrases. An example of each has been circled for you. Read through the paragraph and circle one more example of each.

Later that day, she **suddenly** felt very tired. She rubbed her eyes and sluggishly stretched. It had been a long night waiting for the email finally to arrive. She had woken up **so early that morning**, excited that this could be the day that she got the job. Then she heard it – ping! Trembling with anticipation, she clicked on the message and read it very carefully. There it was! 'We would like to offer you the job!' She read the rest, as quickly as possible, and slowly smiled.

/3

Adverbs in context

Extract from *Life of Pi* by Yann Martel

A young Indian man, Pi Patel, has been shipwrecked in a rowing boat in the Pacific Ocean. Here he is rationing his food intake to ensure his survival.

As the cartons of survival rations diminished, I reduced my intake till I was following the instructions exactly, holding myself to only two biscuits every eight hours. I was continuously hungry. I thought about food obsessively. The less I had to eat, the larger became the portions I dreamed of. My fantasy meals grew to be the size of India. A **Ganges** of **dhal soup**. Hot **chappatis** the size of **Rajasthan**. Bowls of rice as big as **Uttar Pradesh**. **Sambars** to flood all of **Tamil Nadu**. Ice cream heaped as high as the Himalayas. My dreaming became quite expert: all ingredients for my dishes were always in fresh and plentiful supply; the oven or frying pan was always at just the right temperature; the proportion of things was always bang on; nothing was ever burnt or undercooked, nothing too hot or cold. Every meal was simply perfect – only just beyond the reach of my hands.

By degrees the range of my appetite increased. Whereas at first I gutted fish and peeled their skin **fastidiously**, soon I no more than rinsed off their slimy slipperiness before biting into them, delighted to have such a treat between my teeth.

Ganges river that runs through India and Pakistan
dhal soup an Indian lentil soup
chappatis Indian bread
Rajasthan north-west Indian state
Uttar Pradesh north Indian state
sambars Indian stews
Tamil Nadu south Indian state
fastidiously very concerned with accuracy

Activity 1 Understanding the text

a) What is the character doing in lines 1–4?

---

b) How often does he eat the two biscuits? Why does he do that?

---

c) What does the character 'fantasise' about in paragraph 1?

d) In your own words, summarise what the character is doing differently with food in paragraph 2.

Activity 2 Exploring the writer's technique

a) What does the adverb 'exactly' (line 2) tell us about how the character acted?

b) The writer has used the adverb 'obsessively' at the end of the sentence: 'I thought about food obsessively.' Now look at this version: 'I thought obsessively about food.'

Why do you think the writer chose to put the adverb at the end of the sentence?

c) The adverb 'always' is repeated three times in lines 8–10. What is the effect of this?

d) In the following sentence, what does the adverb 'simply' tell us about his imagined meals? 'Every meal was simply perfect.'

Activity 3 Try it yourself

Imagine you've been stranded on a desert island. On a separate piece of paper, use the checklist below to write a description of your first day.

- when the action happened
- where the action happened
- how the action happened
- how much the action happened
- how often the action happened
- how long the action happened
- opinion on the action.

8 Single-clause sentences

What are single-clause sentences?

A single-clause sentence, or simple sentence, is a sentence that contains just one main clause.

A **main clause** is a complete thought, and it makes sense on its own. It can be a single-clause sentence or a clause in a **multi-clause sentence**.

How do they work?

A main clause contains a subject (noun or pronoun) and a verb that refers directly to the subject. It can stand alone as a sentence. Every sentence must contain a main clause for it to be a sentence.

In a main clause, the verb must refer to the subject, and create a complete idea. 'Wendy ice cream' is not a complete thought. It does not contain a verb to explain how Wendy is linked to the ice cream. Did Wendy love ice cream or did Wendy hate ice cream? It is unclear as the verb is missing.

A single-clause sentence can be used to build tension.

The clock struck 1 a.m. I listened. There was the noise again. This time it was closer.	The young woman looked up. She smiled. Jasper flushed red. She'd finally noticed him.

A single-clause sentence can make a clear statement.

I threw the ball.	Rude people are my biggest annoyance.

Subject and object

The subject of an active verb is who or what is doing something. It is often the noun, noun phrase or pronoun that comes before the verb.

Some sentences will also have an object. The object is the person or thing to whom the verb is being done. Usually the object is the noun, noun phrase or pronoun that comes after the verb.

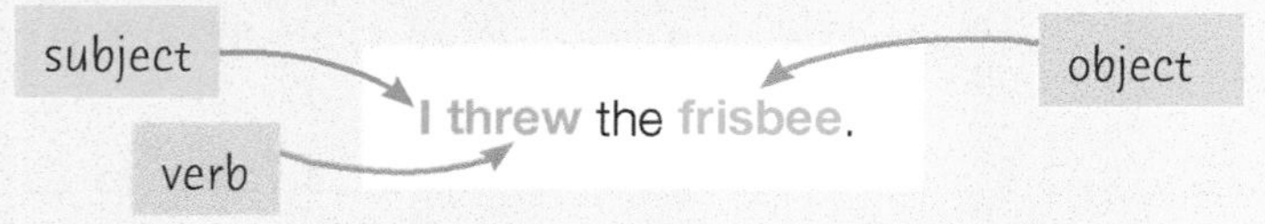

Key terms

main clause a clause that contains a subject and a verb, and makes sense on its own

multi-clause sentence a sentence made up of more than one clause, each with its own verb; they can include two main clauses, or one main clause and one subordinate clause

Tip

Single-clause sentences do not have to be short. They must contain a subject and a verb, but they may also contain an object and various phrase,s such as prepositional phrases, noun phrases and adverbials.

Activity 1

Underline the subject and circle the verb in the following single-clause sentences.

a) Polly was a colourful parrot.

b) We lost our keys.

c) All hope was gone.

d) Unpleasant people are not welcome in this house at any time.

e) Was I alone?

/5

Activity 2

Underline the subject and circle the object in the following single clause sentences.

a) She gave me the cake.

b) Rose passed the ball.

c) I smiled at him.

d) Did Ali really need such a huge meal at the end of the day?

e) The clock struck midnight.

/10

Activity 3

Write each of the following sentences as two single-clause sentences.

Adam was not happy; he had lost his dinner money.

Understanding science is important because it helps us to understand the world.

The ball hit him hard and it hurt.

A new phone is out of the question – we're broke!

Buy your own lunch but use my account.

/5

Single-clause sentences in context

Extract from *Rivers: A Voyage into the Heart of Britain* by Griff Rhys Jones

In the following extract, Griff Rhys Jones describes his experience of swimming in the River Tay in November with the oldest open-water swimming club in Scotland. He is part of a relay exercise with a man called Frank.

My breath came in short rasping gasps. I felt light-headed. I felt that my arms had no power in them. The cold began as a blistering pain and then got worse. I had fully intended to do the crawl but I simply couldn't. I couldn't bring myself to force my head under the water, so I swam down the river using breaststroke. I very rarely
5 swim breaststroke. It usually seems such a slow and clumsy way of **propulsion**, but now, like an old woman with a new hairdo, I kept my turtle head stretched out of the freezing water. [...]

On we went. I have been in cold water before, but this water never warmed me. My thrashing didn't generate heat. I never got used to the cold. It simply got colder
10 and colder and colder. It was sucking the body heat out of me.

The last few minutes were the worst. I thought of sailors on the **North Atlantic convoys**. I thought of the passengers on the *Titanic*. I thought of giving up. If you fall in the North Sea, even in summer, the **hypothermia** will kill you in an hour. The current was not at its fastest on my bit of the relay. My bit turned out to be the
15 longest leg. Frank had made a little miscalculation. I was in the Tay for more like ten minutes and when I came to drag myself out over the edge of the **RIB** my poor red thighs pulled across the rubber like a windscreen scraper.

propulsion the process of driving something forwards

North Atlantic convoys groups of supply boats during World War Two

hypothermia the condition of having an abnormally low body temperature

RIB a type of light, high-performance boat (short for Rigid-hulled Inflatable Boat)

Activity 1 Understanding the text

a) How does Rhys Jones feel in the freezing water?

---

b) What kind of swimming stroke does he use and why?

---

c) What does he think about while he is swimming?

---

d) How long is he in the water?

Activity 2 Exploring the writer's technique

a) Identify three single-clause sentences in the first paragraph. Why do you think that the writer has chosen to use these single-clause sentences instead of a longer construction? Think about how he wants to convey his physical reaction to the cold water.

---

b) The second paragraph begins with a very short single-clause sentence. Rank the following interpretations of why the sentence is effective, using 1 to show the statement you most agree with:

- [ ] It conveys the situation very clearly.
- [ ] It emphasises the writer's feelings that he has no choice but to continue.
- [ ] It implies that the writer is determined and optimistic.

Explain your first choice.

---

c) Look again at the following sentences: 'I thought of sailors on the North Atlantic convoys. I thought of the passengers on the *Titanic*. I thought of giving up.'

What rhetorical technique is the writer using here to convey the writer's feelings? How do the single-clause sentences add to the effect?

---

d) Underline a single-clause sentence in the last paragraph which conveys the writer's sense of humour about his experience. Explain how the simplicity of the sentence adds to the effect.

Activity 3 Try it yourself

Write about a time when something dramatic happened to you. It might be a physical challenge, an accident or a surprise party. Include a number of single-clause sentences to help convey a sense of surprise or shock. You could also include repetition for effect at some point in your writing.

9 Multi-clause sentences (compound)

What are multi-clause sentences?

There are two main types of multi-clause sentence: compound sentences and complex sentences. Compound sentences contain two main clauses that are joined by a **coordinating conjunction**. Each main clause in a compound sentence is of equal importance.

How do they work?

The sentence in the example below contains two main clauses.

main clause → I opened the cupboard and I grabbed my boots. ← main clause

coordinating conjunction: and

If these two sentences were separated with a full stop instead of 'and' they would still make sense on their own.

I opened the cupboard. I grabbed my boots.

In order to show that the two ideas are equal, a coordinating conjunction can be used to join the main clauses together. An easy way of remembering the coordinating conjunctions is to use the **acronym** FANBOYS:

For (to give a reason): for example, 'Rolf approached the safe with caution, for he knew that there were sensors all over the room.'

And (to add): for example, 'I wandered into the room and I felt her eyes on me.'

Nor (to introduce the final set of negative possibilities): for example, 'She couldn't eat the cake, nor could she have any more coffee.'

But (to introduce an alternative): for example, 'I like my teacher, but she is really strict.'

Or (to introduce possibilities): for example, 'We could get a caravan next week or we could go camping.'

Yet (to introduce an opposite): for example, 'Eddie was tired, yet he just couldn't sleep.'

So (to give a consequence): for example, 'I wanted to win, so I ran faster.'

Key terms

acronym a word formed by the initial letters of a phrase and pronounced as a word, e.g. NASA stands for the National Aeronautics and Space Administration

coordinating conjunction a conjunction that joins two parts of a sentence that are of equal weight (they are both full clauses), e.g. and, yet or for

Activity 1

Tick the sentences below that are multi-clause sentences.

Zara liked chips and beans.	
Last night I was woken up by a scream outside, so I put my light on.	
The flowers had wilted on the tree but the root seemed to be alive.	
Next year I want to visit either Lahore or Hong Kong.	
Erik was pleased with the dirt bike he'd built, yet he needed to test it to be sure.	

/5

Activity 2

Read the following statements about compound sentences and circle whether they are true or false.

a) Compound sentences must contain a coordinating conjunction. True / False

b) Compound sentences contain two main clauses. True / False

c) Compound sentences must contain a comma. True / False

d) Compound sentences must contain a capital letter. True / False

e) The two ideas in a compound sentence do not make sense when written as two simple sentences. True / False

/5

Activity 3

Rewrite the single-clause sentences in the following paragraph as multi-clause (compound) sentences. Make sure the meaning does not change.

The building loomed over Miss S. She walked confidently towards the entrance. Inside she felt like fainting. She couldn't let 'them' see her nerves. She had to appear in control. She had to get 'them' to confess. Her case against 'them' had begun 3 years ago. Today was the day she had been waiting for. The receptionist smiled blandly at her. She pointed towards the lift. Miss S. knew that she could be making a warning call to 'them'. She slowed down to make them wait for her for a change.

/6

Multi-clause sentences (compound) in context

Extract from *Walks in and Around London* by Uncle Jonathan

Written in 1895, this extract describes the life of a small child living in the East End of London.

A paper Windmill bought for a **farthing**, which mother has squeezed out of her hard earnings, delights that little three-year-old boy as he holds it tightly in his chubby fist. His clothes are ragged and torn, yet I'm sure his mother is kind to him. He has found out that by holding the mill straight in front of him, the wind 5 catches the bright-coloured sails and spins them around till the colours run one into the other and he sees only a rainbow in front of him. So, forgetting the big boots shaking about on his feet, he trots up and down, laughing merrily.

How admiringly one ragged little fellow looks on at the toy! He, poor boy, never had such a toy to make him happy. He likes to see the whizzing wheel, but rougher 10 games amongst the courts and alleys suit him best. He is one of those little urchins who in the dark days of winter startle us with their shrill calls, or who so suddenly appear at our sides begging a '**copper**'. If we speak to him, he will call us 'general' or 'captain', at the same time saluting us while his eyes twinkle roguishly. Poor little chap! Of course he gets a copper, for his life is a hard one. He dares not creep in to 15 rest at night until the gin palaces are shut, and he knows his parents are sleeping their drunken sleep.

farthing very low-value coin

copper coin

Activity 1 Understanding the text

a) Who buys the boy the windmill?

---

b) What happens to the colours in the windmill when the wind blows?

---

c) What two names does the urchin use to address the writer and his friends?

---

d) Why doesn't the urchin go home until very late?

Activity 2 Exploring the writer's technique

a) Why does the writer use the coordinating conjunction 'yet' in the following multi-clause sentence? 'His clothes are ragged and torn, yet I'm sure his mother is kind to him.'

---

b) What does the main clause sentence 'He likes to see the whizzing wheel, but rougher games amongst the courts and alleys suit him best' tell us about the boy?

---

c) Why has the writer chosen to write the sentence 'Of course he gets a copper, for his life is a hard one' as a multi-clause one and not two single-clause sentences?

---

d) The writer ends with the compound sentence 'He dares not creep in to rest at night until the gin palaces are shut, and he knows his parents are sleeping their drunken sleep.' What is the effect of this on the reader?

Activity 3 Try it yourself

Write a short letter to the local MP explaining the life of this child, and asking him or her for financial support. Add any information that might be relevant, but not mentioned in this extract, for example, other brothers and sisters; living arrangements; school; criminal activity. Try to use some compound sentences in your writing. Once you have completed your letter, read through it and underline or highlight the compound sentences.

10 Multi-clause sentences (complex)

What are complex sentences?

A complex sentence is a type of multi-clause sentence that contains one main clause and at least one **subordinate clause**.

How do they work?

A main clause makes sense on its own. Like a main clause, a subordinate clause also contains a subject and verb, but it cannot make sense on its own. A subordinate clause can be placed at the beginning, the middle or at the end of a sentence. It provides extra information about any part of the main clause.

Although it had been a quiet night, the restaurant remained open in case a customer appeared.

subordinate clause

The subordinate clause 'although it had been a quiet night' gives us extra information about the time of day and the lack of customers. It does not make sense without the main clause.

A subordinate clause will often begin with a **subordinating conjunction**.

Subordinating conjunctions					
after	even if	provided that	that	whenever	while
although	even though	rather than	though	where	why
as	if	since	unless	wherever	
because	in order that	so that	until	whereas	
before	once	than	when	whether	

Relative clauses

A subordinate clause that starts with a relative pronoun is called a relative clause. The relative pronouns are: that, which, whose, whom, who.

The boy, whose brother was swimming much further out, waded in nervously.

relative clause

The relative clause 'whose brother was swimming much further out' gives us extra information about the boy's brother. It does not make sense without the main clause.

Key terms

subordinate clause a clause that adds information to a main clause but can't work as a sentence on its own

subordinating conjunction a word or phrase that joins a less important part of a sentence (subordinate clause) to the most important part of the sentence (main clause), e.g. 'because', 'until', 'whereas'

The boy, **whose brother was swimming much further out**, waded in nervously.

Activity 1

Circle the subordinating conjunction in the sentences below.

a) He walked all the way home because he missed the bus.

b) Before they got on the plane, they had to wait in the departure lounge.

c) She liked playing with her friends rather than doing her homework.

d) Even though it was late, she still really wanted to finish her book.

e) They ran over to help when they saw the child fall over.

f) Once he had tried pineapple pizza he didn't want to eat anything else.

/6

Activity 2

Rewrite the following paragraph to include at least two complex sentences.

The pair walked quickly along the pavement. They paused under the streetlight. They looked around. All was quiet. Then they heard the sound. Mr J.'s mobile was ringing. He stared at the screen. He looked at Mr B. and nodded. This was the call they had been waiting for.

/4

Activity 3

Add a subordinate clause to each main clause to give extra information.

a) The bus swerved, --

----

b) Fredrick saw the figure moving --

----

c) She hears the birds calling a love song to each other --

----

d) He jumped over the fence and dashed towards the blazing building --

----

/4

Multi-clause sentences (complex) in context

Extract from 'The Phantom Coach' by Amelia B. Edwards

In this extract from a short story, published in 1852, the narrator has lost his way on a remote moor in the north of England in December.

Meanwhile, the snow began to come down with **ominous** steadiness, and the wind fell. After this, the cold became more intense, and the night came rapidly up. As for me, my **prospects** darkened with the darkening sky, and my heart grew heavy as I thought how my young wife was already watching for me through the window of 5 our little inn **parlour**, and thought of all the suffering in store for her throughout this weary night. We had been married four months, and, having spent our autumn in the Highlands, were now lodging in a remote little village situated just on the verge of the great English moorlands. We were very much in love, and, of course, very happy. This morning, when we parted, she had **implored** me to return before 10 dusk, and I had promised her that I would. What would I not have given to have kept my word!

Even now, weary as I was, I felt that with a supper, an hour's rest, and a guide, I might still get back to her before midnight, if only guide and shelter could be found.

And all this time, the snow fell and the night thickened. I stopped and shouted every 15 now and then, but my shouts seemed only to make the silence deeper.

ominous menacing, suggesting that something bad it going to happen

prospects chances of success

parlour front room

implored begged

Activity 1 Understanding the text

a) What is the weather like as the narrator walks across the moor?

---

b) Who is the narrator concerned about and why?

---

c) What does the narrator hope to find?

---

d) What does the narrator do to try and help him find his way?

Activity 2 Exploring the writer's technique

a) Look again at the multi-clause sentence beginning, 'As for me...' in line 2. What does the subordinate clause 'as I thought how my young wife was already watching for me through the window of our little inn parlour' suggest about the relationship between the narrator and his wife?

---

b) What does the subordinate clause, 'having spent our autumn in the Highlands' provide the reader with?

---

c) What is the effect of the subordinate clause 'if only guide and shelter could be found' in line 13? Think about the narrator's attitude to his situation and how he would be feeling at this point.

---

d) The narrator says, 'I stopped and shouted every now and then, but my shouts seemed only to make the silence deeper.' Using the subordinating conjunction 'Even though', rewrite this sentence with a subordinate clause at the start. Which version do you prefer and why?

Activity 3 Try it yourself

Think of an outdoor place you know well, for example a park or local attraction. Write a short guide to this place. Use some multi-clause sentences in your guide, including subordinate clauses such as:

- Although some people may not enjoy being outside, ...
- ...., even if it is pouring with rain.
- ...., whenever you can.

11 Paragraphs

What are paragraphs?

A paragraph is a group of sentences that share a common idea.

How do they work?

A new paragraph is used every time there is a significant change in the text, for example, a new speaker. Paragraphs are used to help the reader make sense of a piece of writing. They group sentences together so ideas are easier to follow.

Paragraphs often start with a topic sentence that introduces the main idea. The sentences that follow then add more detail.

To show where a new paragraph starts, you can either indent the first line or leave a line space between paragraphs.

There are five rules for starting a new paragraph in a piece of writing. The acronym TiPToPD is a helpful way to remember the rules.

Ti – a new time is introduced

Last night, I was so tired that I literally fell asleep with my phone in my hand. I had had a rotten day at work; there were so many emergency callouts that we barely had time to sit, let alone eat. I eventually got to bed at around 3 a.m., and when I checked my phone I had so many messages to read.

This morning, things were a bit calmer...

P – a new place is introduced

Our living room is cream with a huge family photograph on the shelf. My mum refuses to take it down as she says it's a bit of history – more like a bit of embarrassment if you ask me!

Our kitchen is large and modern. It has a wooden floor, and we have one of those cool American fridge-freezers that makes ice...

To – a new topic is introduced

I feel that work experience is valuable time spent away from school. Previous students have reported that the single greatest gain was their increased confidence. They felt that the time spent away from their studies was worth it.

Teachers had a very different opinion on the matter...

P – a new person begins to speak

"I'm sorry, but I can't hear you. I think it must be the signal!" I called.

"What about now?" she replied.

"It's better," I answered.

"Now?" she asked.

"I'll call you back later!" I shouted.

D – for dramatic effect

The house loomed over the man as he looked up at the bare windows and the weathered door. It had been years since he had been here. Twenty? Thirty? He shivered. It was cold but that wasn't it; he knew exactly what had caused it – being back here again after he'd vowed never to return. And yet he couldn't stop thinking about it. It drew him.

This house had secrets that he needed to know.

Activity 1

Read the following statements about paragraphs and circle whether they are true or false.

a) If you are writing about animals in a zoo, you could start a new paragraph when you start writing about a new animal. True / False

b) A paragraph must contain six sentences. True / False

c) A topic sentence often starts a paragraph. True / False

d) An indentation is where you leave a line between paragraphs. True / False

e) You need a new paragraph if you start writing about a new setting in your story. True / False

f) If I wrote a paragraph about Saturday, I would need a new one to write about Sunday. True / False

/6

Activity 2

Read the following text and use a double forward slash // to show where new paragraphs should begin. There should be four paragraphs

As the sun rose, I could hear the noise of the men outside our tent readying our breakfast, and the horses beginning to move around. I slowly rolled over in my sleeping bag and smiled. I couldn't believe the day had finally come. Today was the day we would take our horses across the Sahara Desert. After a light breakfast, we were guided over to our horses. We were encouraged to 'make friends' by stroking them and talking to them. My new 'friend' was a silky, chocolate-coloured beast. I am not a horse person generally, but this fine animal was something to admire. Harsh fabric scratched my skin as I clambered on top and tried to get comfortable for the long trek. I glanced around, taking in the sight of my fellow travellers in various states of horse mounting. At the front of the line, my horse strode confidently on, tethered by the anchoring rope between master and servant. I felt a pang of sympathy for my carrier, his mouth being pulled along by the seemingly hardened owner. As the day wore on, the buildings seemed to fall away and suddenly we were in the expansive Sahara Desert – dust and mountains in front, as far as the eye could see. The vastness was immeasurable: stretching far beyond the eye into the future.

/4

12 Cohesive devices

What are cohesive devices?

A cohesive device is a linking word, phrase or sentence. It can be placed at the start of a sentence and between words, phrases and sentences.

> Firstly, we'll visit the market and you can buy some local produce.
>
> Then, we'll explore the old town.

How do they work?

The following table gives examples of some of the more common cohesive devices. You may recognise some of them as coordinating or subordinating conjunctions.

Adding	Explaining	Sequencing	Illustrating
also and another furthermore in addition	as a result of because consequently due to so therefore thus	after finally firstly, secondly in conclusion next then ultimately	as shown in namely for example such as

Comparing	Contrasting	Highlighting	Reframing
as with equally likewise similarly	but conversely however instead on the contrary on the other hand unlike	especially in particular notably	in other words put simply that is to say

Find out more

See pages 34–37 for more about coordinating conjunctions and pages 38–41 for more about subordinating conjunctions.

Firstly, we'll visit the market **and** you can buy some local produce.

Activity 1

Read the following paragraph and underline the four cohesive devices.

My position on Instagram is very clear. Firstly, it is a time-waster that provides users with the 'best bits' of other people's lives and leads to people feeling under pressure to have what they perceive to be the perfect life – put simply it should be renamed 'bragstagram'. For example, users see photographs of the perfect 'holiday' scene – people smiling, sipping cocktails in the sun, looking tanned and happy. While some would see this as threatening, those of us who understand what holidays are really like, however, know that the truth is very different.

/4

Activity 2

Add the following cohesive devices to the sentences below.

for example | however | then | in addition | therefore | in particular

a) My grandmother loves cooking Italian food, ____________________ lasagne with added chilli.

b) I can't wait to get in and relax in the evenings, _________ I also like to make sure I exercise at least three times a week.

c) Lennie in *Of Mice and Men* is a strong but childish character, ____________ when he wants to pet the rabbits but accidentally squashes one.

d) Head office has informed us that they are going to redecorate our offices, starting with the main office, __________ the meeting rooms followed by the kitchen and toilets.

e) Cadence did not complete her code-breaking training this week, ___________ she now needs to attend a catch-up session along with her hostage negotiation training.

f) _______________ to her normal 13 girls training tonight, there will also be two new girls who are going to try out.

/6

Activity 3

Read the following arguments for and then against computer gaming. Use cohesive devices to write sentences that contrast the different sides. Write your sentences on separate paper.

For:

- hand–eye coordination is improved
- problem-solving skills are enhanced
- making friends through online gaming facilities

Against:

- time-waster
- talking to strangers through online gaming facilities
- violent scenes are presented to young and impressionable people

/6

Cohesive devices in context

Extract from *Learn About the Basics of Pop-Up Restaurants* by Lorri Mealey, 2017

The following text is taken from an internet advice article for people considering opening a pop-up restaurant.

What's on a Pop-Up Restaurant Menu?

People go to a pop-up restaurant to experience a unique, creative eating experience. Therefore, your pop-up restaurant menu should be original-something you can't find at any local eateries. Due to the limited nature of most pop-up kitchens, a **prix fixe** menu or limited menu is ideal. Some pop-up restaurants offer a five, six or seven-course meal-no choices allowed. 5

Some Problems with Pop-Ups

A pop-up restaurant is a lot like catering a large event, except that it goes on for days, weeks or even months. You need to plan the logistics carefully. For example, how are you going to keep food warm and/or cold before and during the dinner rush? Other **logistics** to consider is transportation of supplies and equipment and knowing how much food to buy for each night. 10

... Pop-Ups Should Be Legit

Truly underground pop-up restaurants don't usually bother with licenses or insurance. However, you need both to be legal and avoid any potential legal trouble if problems should arise. 15

... Don't Overlook Safety for Your Pop-Up

First and foremost, your pop-up location should be safe for **patrons** and safe to serve food. If electricity and running water aren't readily available, you need to make sure you have access to both for extended periods of time. Food needs to be kept in the safe temperature zones for hot and cold, to avoid any possible food poisoning. 20

prix-fixe - fixed price

logistics - the organising of everything involved in a large operation

patrons - customers

Activity 1 Understanding the text

a) In your own words, explain why people go to a pop-up restaurant.

---

b) What is the best kind of menu for a pop-up?

---

c) List two things which someone opening a pop-up needs to think about.

---

d) What do you think is the most important thing to remember if you are setting up a pop-up? Explain why.

Activity 2 Exploring the writer's technique

a) Reread the sentences: 'People go to a pop-up restaurant to experience a unique, creative eating experience. Therefore, your pop-up restaurant menu should be original – something you can't find at any local eateries.'

How does the word 'therefore' help to link these two points?

---

b) In the third paragraph the writer uses the word 'However'.

- What other cohesive word or phrase could be used here? Rewrite the sentence using this word or phrase.

- Which version of the sentence do you prefer and why?

---

c) Which cohesive device emphasises the writer's point in the last paragraph? Why is this phrase particularly effective?

Activity 3 Try it yourself

Think of something you love to eat which would be suitable for a local pop-up restaurant. Write an email to this pop-up explaining why this dish would work well, using cohesive devices to help you convey your ideas. You might include:

- Because it is quick to make, ...
- For example, this dish would be popular with....
- As a result, customers would ......
- Furthermore, people would be likely to tell....

1 Capital letters

What are capital letters?

A capital letter is the upper-case version of a letter, for example, 'R', 'T' or 'A'. A capital letter goes at the start of a sentence. It is also used to show that a word is a proper noun.

How do they work?

Starting a sentence

A capital letter is used every time you start a new sentence.

The boat rattled as the waves hit it with their full force. Like a toy in the hands of a small child, it rocked uncontrollably with no control or power to stop what was happening. It was like the waves were exacting revenge on the vessel.

Proper nouns

A capital letter is used for every proper noun. This includes days of the week, months, festivals, places, people's names, organisations, brands, political parties and sporting clubs, religious figures and holy books.

Mrs Bradford   Liverpool Football Club   Halloween

Titles

The title of a book, film, play, short story, poem, essay, etc. should always start with a capital letter and should include capital letters for nouns, verbs, adverbs and adjectives. Words like 'a', 'an', 'and', 'in', 'one', 'to', and 'the' do not need capital letters unless they come at the start of a title.

The Cat in the Hat   *A Long Walk to Freedom*   'War Photographer'

Abbreviations

If you are writing an abbreviation of a longer phrase, each letter should be capitalised.

BBC (British Broadcasting Corporation)   GCSE (General Certificate of Secondary Education)   USA (United States of America)

Find out more

See pages 4–5 for more about nouns.

The boat rattled as the waves hit it with their full force.

Activity 1

Read the following statements about capital letters and circle whether they are true or false.

a) Capital letters are used for all nouns. True / False

b) Days of the week start with a capital letter. True / False

c) TV should have capital letters. True / False

d) The school subject English should start with a capital letter. True / False

e) Capital letters are used for all proper nouns. True / False

f) Football teams should not start with capital letters. True / False

/6

Activity 2

Rewrite each of these titles using capital letters in the correct places.

a) the hunger games (novel)

----

b) britain's got talent (TV show)

----

c) happy birthday (song)

----

d) the very hungry caterpillar (children's book)

----

e) snow white and the huntsman (film)

----

f) a sound of thunder (short story)

/6

Activity 3

Read the paragraph below and circle the letters that should be capitalised.

the train left warsaw for the city of gdansk at 11.35 a.m. on tuesday 11th june. elena nowak knew the exact time and date as this was the day that would change her life – forever. as she gazed out at the polish countryside, she thought about her father. she had never met him. her mother, julia, had told her so little about him (she only knew his name was max kowal and that he was from a small village near gdansk called kartuzy) that she had created her own version of him. he was tall, with a warm smile and dark hair – like her but different. she smiled; soon she would know the truth.

/20

Tip

Practise using capital letters correctly when you send text messages and emails. It's a bad habit to use only lower case – challenge yourself!

Capital letters in context

Extract from *Oranges are Not the Only Fruit* by Jeanette Winterson

In this extract, the main character, Jeanette, describes her mother's strict religious character through her likes and dislikes. The author uses capital letters in a non-conventional way. You will think about the reasons for this as you work through the activities.

Like most people I lived for a long time with my mother and father. My father liked to watch the wrestling, my mother liked to wrestle; it didn't matter what. She was in the white corner and that was that.

She hung out the largest sheets on the windiest days. She *wanted* the **Mormons**
5 to knock on the door. At election times in a Labour mill town she put a picture of the Conservative candidate in the window.

She had never heard of mixed feelings. There were friends and there were enemies.

Enemies were: The Devil (in his many forms)
Next Door
10 Sex (in its many forms)
Slugs
Friends were: God
Our dog
Auntie Madge
15 The novels of Charlotte Brontë
Slug pellets

and me, at first, I had been brought in to join her in a tag match against the Rest of the World.

Mormons a religious and cultural group

Activity 1 Understanding the text

a) Who does the narrator live with?

----

b) What does her father watch?

----

c) What does her mother do on the 'windiest days'?

d) Why are 'Slugs' and 'Slug pellets' placed in different categories?

Activity 2 Exploring the writer's technique

a) Why does the writer use a capital letter for 'Mormons'?

b) Why do you think the writer has chosen to start all of the words or phrases in the categories 'enemies' and 'friends' with a capital letter?

c) Why do 'dog' and 'pellets' not start with a capital letter?

d) The title of the novel is *Oranges are Not the Only Fruit*. Why is 'Not' *not* considered an 'in between' word and instead starts with a capital letter?

Activity 3 Try it yourself

Write a newspaper article about an alien sighting. Include:

- what happened and when it happened
- two eyewitness accounts
- how the government plans to protect us from an invasion
- advice to readers if they spot the alien.

Remember to use capital letters correctly throughout your article.

2 Full stops, exclamation marks, question marks

What are full stops, exclamation marks and question marks?

Full stops, exclamation marks and question marks are punctuation marks. An exclamation mark and a question mark are generally placed at the end of a sentence. A full stop is placed in a number of places, but most commonly at the end of a sentence.

How do full stops work?

A full stop (.) is used at the end of a sentence. It is not needed at the end of every clause. This is because two or more clauses can be found in a sentence.

> The cat was tired after chasing the dog. Therefore, it padded over to its basket and lay down. It quickly fell asleep.

See pages 34–41 for more about multi-clause sentences.

How do exclamation marks work?

An exclamation mark (!) is used to express a strong emotion or a sense of drama. It shows that the sentence would be exclaimed, shouted, or said with emphasis or deep feeling.

> Please help me!
>
> What an amazing view!

How do question marks work?

A question mark is used to indicate the end of a question.

> Could you pass me the hot sauce, please?
>
> How many are there?

Reported speech, or indirect speech, is when you recount what someone says without using the exact words.You do not need a question mark if the question is within reported speech.

> He asked me to pass the hot sauce.
>
> She asked how many there were.

The cat was tired after chasing the dog.

Activity 1

Add a full stop, exclamation mark or question mark to the following sentences so the meaning is clear.

a) Boris climbed the ladder slowly so he wouldn't fall off

b) Would you adopt an abandoned animal who needed a home

c) The sun sank, turning the sky a pale pink as it disappeared

d) Please would you stop shouting at me

e) What time will the helicopter take off

f) Look out for that falling branch

/6

Activity 2

Read the conversation below and insert either an exclamation mark or a question mark.

"Could I arrange a meeting with you regarding the issue at lunchtime_____" asked Mr Ben.

"What_____ I didn't do anything_____" Sophie shouted.

"Do you think that's the way you should be talking to a member of staff_____"

"But you are accusing me of doing something I haven't done_____"

"I'm asking you, were you throwing potato wedges in the cafeteria_____"

"No_____"

"Are you sure_____"

"Yes_____"

/9

Activity 3

Read the following statements about full stops, exclamation marks and question marks. Circle whether they are true or false.

a) Full stops are used at the end of every clause. True / False

b) Website addresses do not need full stops. True / False

c) Sentences that begin with 'who' need a question mark. True / False

d) Exclamation marks are only used in speech. True / False

e) Exclamation marks can show anger in a sentence. True / False

/5

Full stops, exclamation marks and question marks in context

Extract from *A Study in Scarlet* by Arthur Conan Doyle

This novel was published in 1887. It is the first of the Sherlock Holmes mysteries. Here, Holmes is showing Dr Watson his latest scientific discovery.

"Dr. Watson, Mr. Sherlock Holmes," said Stamford, introducing us.

"How are you?" he said **cordially**, gripping my hand with a strength for which I should hardly have given him credit. "You have been in Afghanistan, I perceive."

"How on earth did you know that?" I asked in astonishment.

5 "Never mind," said he, chuckling to himself. "The question now is about **haemoglobin**. No doubt you see the significance of this discovery of mine?"

"It is interesting, chemically, no doubt," I answered, "but practically –"

"Why, man, it is the most practical **medico-legal** discovery for years. Don't you see that it gives us an infallible test for bloodstains? Come over here now!" He
10 seized me by the coat-sleeve in his eagerness, and drew me over to the table at which he had been working. "Let us have some fresh blood," he said, digging a long **bodkin** into his finger, and drawing off the resulting drop of blood in a chemical pipette ... In an instant the contents assumed a dull mahogany colour, and a brownish dust was precipitated to the bottom of the glass jar.

15 "Ha! ha!" he cried, clapping his hands, and looking as delighted as a child with a new toy. "What do you think of that?"

"It seems to be a very delicate test," I remarked.

"Beautiful! beautiful! The old **Guiacum test** was very clumsy and uncertain. So is the microscopic examination for blood **corpuscles**. The latter is valueless if the
20 stains are a few hours old. Now, this appears to act as well whether the blood is old or new. Had this test been invented, there are hundreds of men now walking the earth who would long ago have paid the penalty of their crimes."

"Indeed!" I murmured.

cordially in a friendly manner

haemoglobin a red protein which moves oxygen in blood

medico-legal describing something that has both medical and legal aspects

bodkin a blunt needle with a large eye

Guiacum test one of the first methods of testing for blood in forensic (criminal) science

corpuscles tiny cells or bodies in an organism

Activity 1 Understanding the text

a) Which two people are meeting for the first time?

b) What does Sherlock do to his finger?

c) What test is called "very clumsy and uncertain"?

d) What question does Watson ask?

Key term

rhetorical question a question asked without expecting an answer. It is often used to make an important point, e.g. 'Are you kidding me?'

Activity 2 Exploring the writer's technique

a) Why does the sentence "Come over here now!" end with an exclamation mark?

b) What do Holmes' exclamations "Beautiful! beautiful!" in line 17 tell us about his thoughts on his new experiment?

c) How does the writer show that Holmes is "as delighted as a child with a new toy"?

d) Explain why Holmes uses **rhetorical questions** such as "Don't you see that it gives us an infallible test for bloodstains?" in line 8.

Activity 3 Try it yourself

Write a conversation between two people. One person should be asking for directions, but he or she keeps getting confused. The other person is trying to give directions, and he or she is getting frustrated. Make sure you use correct punctuation throughout.

3 Apostrophes

What are apostrophes?

An apostrophe is a punctuation mark with two roles: to show possession (belonging) or to show that letters are missing (omission).

How do they work?

Possession

An apostrophe is used to show that something belongs to someone or something. If something belongs to just one person or thing, add an apostrophe followed by **-s** at the end of the word.

It was Sunjita's eagle.

In this sentence, the eagle belongs to Sunjita. She is the owner.

If the owner's name ends in **-s**, you can either put an apostrophe after the **-s** or you can add an **-s** with an apostrophe before it.

It was Jess's idea to go to Greece.   James' hair was unusual.

Plural nouns that end in **-s** only need an apostrophe after the **-s** that is already there.

The nurses' station

This tells us that the station belongs to more than one nurse.

Plural nouns that do not end in **-s** need an apostrophe and **-s**.

The Women's FA Cup Final was held at Wembley.

Omission

An apostrophe is used when two words are combined to create a shortened (contracted) word.

should not = shouldn't   we have = we've   it is = it's

It's/Its

Make sure you don't confuse the following:

- Use 'its' when you want to show possession. Do not add an apostrophe.
- Use 'it's' as a contraction of 'it is' or 'it has'.

possession: the nest belongs to the bird

contraction: 'it is' or 'it has'

The bird flew back to its nest.

It's been a lovely day.

Activity 1

Place a tick in the box next to the sentences where the apostrophes have been used correctly.

I can't remember how I ended up in this mess.	
My dads sister is a professional cricketer.	
Yan went to the men's section to look for a pink shirt.	
England's second largest city is Birmingham.	
The birthday present's from my brother were the worst!	

/5

Tip

Not every word ending in 's' needs an apostrophe. Learn the rules so you don't get into the bad habit of adding one to every word ending in 's'.

Activity 2

Write the correct uncontracted form of the following words.

a) don't ....

b) I've ....

c) she's ....

d) we'd ....

e) they're..

f) mustn't ....

g) could've ....

h) we'll ....

/8

Activity 3

Rewrite the following phrases using an apostrophe to show possession. For example, 'the hat owned by the man' should be 'the man's hat'.

a) the fish owned by my stepbrother

....

b) the pens owned by his class

....

c) the key owned by the jailer

....

d) the toys owned by the children

....

e) the rooms owned by the hotel

....

f) the bananas owned by the monkeys

....

/6

4 Commas

What are commas?

A comma is used to separate information. It indicates a pause and helps to communicate the natural rhythm of a sentence.

How do they work?

Separating clauses

Commas can be used in multi-clause sentences to separate a main clause and any subordinate clauses. Commas help make the meaning of the sentence clear.

Ben was exhausted, because he had not slept well.

Separating main clauses

Commas are sometimes used before the coordinating conjunction in a multi-clause sentence to separate two main clauses. These are clauses that do not need each other to make sense as they make sense on their own.

main clause 1

I wasn't sure how to get there, but I had a hand-drawn map.

main clause 2

Lists

A comma is used to separate three or more items in a list.

I had carrots, peas, potatoes and onions with my lunch.

The flat had a small, dingy, damp bedroom.

In speech

If direct speech follows information about the speaker, a comma is needed directly before the **inverted commas.**

Elise shouted, "I'm in here!"

A comma is also used after the speech and before the information about the speaker. Remember, the comma should sit inside the speech marks when you are punctuating direct speech.

"It's over there," pointed Tia.

Key term

inverted commas (or speech marks) a punctuation mark that goes at the beginning " and end " of spoken words

Find out more

See pages 64–67 for more about direct speech, pages 34–41 for multi-clause sentences and pages 26–29 for adverbs.

I wasn't sure how to get there, but I had received a hand-drawn map.

After an adverb or adverbial

A comma can be used after an adverb or adverbial that comes at the start of a sentence.

Angrily, he slammed down the telephone.

adverb followed by a comma

Activity 1

Add commas to the following lists.

a) She added the red purple yellow and black paint to the mix.

b) The café's Big Breakfast included fried toast baked beans fried tomatoes and eggs.

c) Hawaii California New York and Florida are American states.

d) Shenay listened to The Beatles Janis Joplin Olly Murs and Ed Sheeran.

e) Albert Teneson had beaten Marcus Krupp Ulana Hotisch and Charles Athleton to make it to the chess final.

f) I won the 100 m sprint 200 m sprint and 4 x 100 m relay at our school sports day.

/6

Activity 2

Tick the sentences where the comma has been used correctly. Where the comma has been used incorrectly, mark where it should go.

The road snaked around the, edge of the cliff crossed the bridge and went into the valley.	
Before she went to sleep that night, Leanna wrote a few pages of her book.	
Without warning, the buildings were hidden behind the approaching dust clouds.	
Just as the traffic light turned red, Andrei managed to pull his horse and cart to a stop.	
Mr Han's wife daughter and son, crossed the border to Laos.	
Ben Nevis, which is in Scotland, is the highest peak in the British Isles.	

/6

Activity 3

Read the paragraph below. Add commas to separate the clauses where you think they are necessary.

Slowly Mrs Eden walked across the field towards the large apple tree and there she found the thing she had been looking for. Covered in leaves dirt and branches was the box that he had left there all those weeks before the accident had happened. Carefully she sat down leaning against the tree for support. She looked down at the old dirty box noticing that it was starting to go mouldy at the edges. 'A bit like me' she said aloud.

/6

5 Parenthesis: brackets, commas and dashes

What is parenthesis?

Parenthesis adds additional information to a sentence. Words in parenthesis are separated from the main clause using commas, brackets or dashes. The plural of parenthesis is parentheses.

How does it work?

Words in parenthesis can add information, an afterthought, a comment or a reference.

Her sister, who stared at me in shock, listened to the confession.

Twitter – a social media communication platform – was created in 2006.

Parentheses separate extra information from the main clause. You should be able to remove the information in parentheses, and the sentence would still make sense.

main clause

India (population 1.5 billion) is located on the Asian continent.

India is located on the Asian continent.

parenthesis

main clause

When deciding whether to use brackets, commas or dashes for parentheses, you need to think about whether your writing is formal or informal. Generally, a dash is used in more informal writing while brackets and commas are considered more formal.

brackets used for more formal writing

We went swimming (the pool was huge) every day.

We went swimming – the pool was huge – every day.

dashes used for more informal writing

Tip

Avoid overusing dashes in your writing. Always think carefully about the most appropriate punctuation.

Activity 1

Add appropriate punctuation for the words which should be in parentheses in the sentences below.

a) The house, which stood beyond the river, had been empty since the invasion.

b) Professor Quartez, who was in charge of the artefacts department, stared at the empty space where the Roman sword should have been.

c) Germany population 83 million is bordered by eight other countries.

d) The designer used Pinterest an online pinboard to gather ideas for the interior of the new hotel.

e) Anya despite her reservations accepted Milo's invitation for a date.

/5

Activity 2

Tick the sentences where parentheses have been used correctly.

The water (from the River Rhine) trickled along the chattering brook.	
As (he finished the performance) Sonny felt elated.	
Ollie and Siena who had been enemies at first sat next to each other (in every lesson).	
Her orders were to follow the old man (Bob) even though she knew he was dangerous.	
The film ended (with the strange disappearance of the main character).	

/5

Activity 3

Read the sentences below then rewrite them, adding a pair of brackets, commas or dashes in the correct place.

a) My friends whom I trust with my darkest secrets knew the truth about what had happened.

---

b) The president who was sitting at his desk couldn't decide what to tweet.

---

c) Munich some say is the best city in the world.

---

d) Every night after she had finished her painting she escaped to the garden.

---

e) Around the corner was the abandoned church everyone said it was haunted and a huge willow tree.

/5

Commas in context

Extract from *Perfect* by Rachel Joyce

The novel was published in 2013. Jim lives alone in a caravan. He suffers from obsessive compulsive disorder, which is a mental health condition where some sufferers feel the need to repeat certain acts. In this extract, he returns to his caravan and begins to perform particular actions in a certain order.

He performs the ritual twenty-one times. That's the number it has to be done. He steps into the caravan. He greets his things. He steps out of the van. In, hello, out. In, hello, out. Locking and unlocking the door every time.

Twenty-one is safe. Nothing will happen if he does it twenty-one times. Twenty is not safe and neither is twenty-two. If something else swings into his mind – an image or a different word – the whole process will begin again. (5)

No one has any idea about this part of Jim's life. On the estate, he straightens the wheelie bins or picks up small items of litter. He says, H-hello, how are you? to the boys at the skate ramp, and he carries the recycling boxes sometimes to help the refuse collectors, and no one would know what he must go through when he is (10) alone. There is a lady with a dog who sometimes asks where he lives, if he would like to join her one day for bingo in the community centre. They have lovely prizes she says; sometimes a meal for two at the pub in town. But Jim makes his excuses.

Once he has finished stepping in and out of the caravan there is more. There will be lying on his stomach to seal the doorframe with duct tape and then the windows, (15) in case of intruders. There will be checking the cupboards and under the pull-up bed and behind the curtain, over and over. Sometimes, even when it is finished, he still doesn't feel safe and the process must begin again, not just with the duct tape, but also with the key. Giddy with tiredness, he steps in and out, locking the door, unlocking it again. Saying Foot Mat hello. Taps hello. (20)

He has had no real friends since he was at school. He has never been with a woman. Since the closure of Besley Hill, he has wished for both, for friends, for love – for knowing and being known – but if you are stepping in and out of doors, and greeting inanimate objects, as well as securing openings with duct tape, there isn't much left over time. Besides, he's often so nervous he can't say the words. (25)

Activity 1 Understanding the text

a) Who is the extract about?

---

b) Where does the character live?

----

c) What does the character 'greet'?

Activity 2 Exploring the writer's technique

a) Why has the writer used a comma in the following sentence 'On the estate, he straightens the wheelie bins or picks up small items of litter'?

----

b) i) The writer has used a pair of dashes in the following sentence. Rewrite it using commas instead of the dashes.

'If something else swings into his mind – an image or a different word – the whole process must begin again.'

----

ii) How does changing the dashes in this sentence to commas change the effect of the sentence?

----

c) In the sentence that follows, the writer has used commas to separate clauses. Why has the writer included this extra information inside the commas for the reader?

'Sometimes, even when it is finished, he still doesn't feel safe and the process must begin again, not just with the duct tape, but also with the key.'

Activity 3 Try it yourself

Imagine you are Rachel Joyce. On separate paper, write, another two paragraphs to finish off the extract on p 62. Make sure that you use commas correctly throughout your paragraphs.

6 Direct speech

What is direct speech?

Direct speech presents the exact words of a speaker. It is most common in fiction writing (for example, a conversation between characters) and in news reports (for example, eyewitness accounts of events).

How does it work?

When using direct speech, there are rules that are followed to ensure that the reader can understand what is being said, by whom and in what way.

1 Every word of the direct speech is placed within inverted commas. These are also known as speech marks.

2 If the direct speech ends with an exclamation mark or question mark, there is no need for a capital letter to begin the speaker information.

3 Information about the speaker goes outside of the inverted commas. It can go before or after the direct speech.

4 Each time a new speaker speaks a new paragraph must be started. A paragraph can be just a short sentence.

5 A comma is used to introduce direct speech if information about the speaker comes before it.

6 When speaker information is placed in the middle of direct speech, a punctuation mark is needed to end the first part of their speech. A full stop or comma is also needed after the speaker information.

7 A comma, full stop, question mark or exclamation mark must follow the direct speech. These are placed inside the inverted commas.

"It can't possibly be true!" she gasped.

"I can assure you it is. He was caught red-handed by the security guard," **the policeman replied.**

She sat down muttering, "I'm in shock."

"I can imagine, ma'am," he said politely. "It must be very difficult to hear that your husband has committed such a crime."

Activity 1

a) Use inverted commas to show which words in the paragraph below are direct speech.

b) Use two forward slashes // to show where a new paragraph for a new speaker should begin.

I can see it over there! she shouted loudly, pointing to the mountain in the distance. Where? I can't see anything, he answered. There, there! she continued to point. He rolled his eyes and sighed, You can keep pointing but I can't see it.

/7

Activity 2

Add the correct punctuation to the conversation below so that it is clear.

You may need to use: commas, full stops, exclamation marks, question marks.

"Lois, can you go up and tidy your bedroom please "

Lois groaned "What now "

"Yes now, it is a tip "

"Can't I do it tomorrow " she asked

"No " Mum replied sternly "You gave me that answer last week and it is still in the same state "

/5

Activity 3

Rewrite the dialogue below, using the speaker information (in bold) to make it an argument between the speakers.

Think about:

- **how you might use adverbs to describe the way it is 'said'**
- **actions that the speakers might do during the conversation.**

"Look, I couldn't get here any quicker!" **said Omar**. ....

"Then you should have left earlier," **said Hanif**. ....

"I left with plenty of time," **said Omar**. .... "I got caught in traffic!"

"What, like last week?" **said Hanif**. .... "And the week before that, and the ..."

"That is very unfair!" **said Omar**. ....

"But true," **said Hanif**. ....

"Oi! Don't get rude!" **said Omar**. ....

"You'll make me late again! I'll be rude if I want to," **said Hanif**. ....

/8

Direct speech in context

Extract from *Persuasion* by Jane Austen

Sir Walter Elliot, a snobbish baronet, has been forced to rent out his family home, Kellynch Hall, to Admiral and Lady Croft, people he believes to be socially inferior to him. He and his daughters, Anne and Elizabeth, are staying in Bath. According to a letter they have just received from Mary, Sir Walter's youngest daughter, the Crofts are now visiting Bath too.

Sir Walter wanted to know whether the Crofts travelled with four horses, and whether they were likely to be situated in such a part of Bath as it might suit Miss Elliot and himself to visit in; but had little curiosity beyond.

"How is Mary?" said Elizabeth; and without waiting for answer, "And pray what brings the Crofts to Bath?" 5

"They come on the Admiral's account. He is thought to be **gouty**."

"**Gout** and **decrepitude**!" said Sir Walter. "Poor old gentleman."

"Have they any **acquaintance** here?" asked Elizabeth.

"I do not know; but I can hardly suppose that, at Admiral Croft's time of life, and in his profession, he should not have many acquaintances in such a place as this." 10

"I suspect," said Sir Walter coolly, "that Admiral Croft will be best known in Bath as the renter of Kellynch Hall. Elizabeth, may we venture to present him and his wife in **Laura Place**?"

"Oh no! I think not. Situated as we are with **Lady Dalrymple**, cousins, we ought to be very careful not to embarrass her with acquaintance she might not approve. If we were not related, it would not signify; but as cousins, she would feel **scrupulous** as to any proposal of ours. We had better leave the Crofts to find their own level. There are several odd-looking men walking about here, who I am told, are sailors. The Crofts will associate with them!" 15

gouty – suffering from the disease gout

gout – a form of arthritis

decrepitude – state of frailty and weakness

Laura Place – the prestigious home of the important

Lady Dalrymple – a relative of the Elliotts

scrupulous – wanting to do the right thing

Activity 1 Understanding the text

a) What information about the Crofts does Sir Walter want? What does this suggest about his attitude to them?

---

b) What is wrong with Admiral Croft?

---

c) Who are the Elliots related to and where does she live?

---

d) Who does Elizabeth think the Crofts should socialise with?

Activity 2 Exploring the writer's technique

a) The first paragraph of this extract is written as reported or indirect speech. Rewrite this paragraph using direct speech, including Sir Walter's questions.

---

b) Elizabeth asks after her sister, Mary. What does the information 'and without waiting for answer' suggest about her?

---

c) Reread the following: "**Gout** and **decrepitude!**" said Sir Walter. "Poor old gentleman."

i) Sir Walter makes an exclamation. What words could be used to replace the word 'said' in this context?

---

ii) Why does the writer uses a full stop rather than a comma before the words Sir Walter speaks next?

---

d) What does the adverb, 'coolly' convey about Sir Walter's feelings towards Admiral Croft?

Activity 3 Try it yourself

Write a conversation between two or three characters about somebody they like and admire. Include information about the speakers and how they convey their ideas. Avoid using the word 'said' too often.

7 Semi-colons

What are semi-colons?

A semi-colon can be used to link two main clauses that are of equal importance, but are closely related. It can also be used to separate longer items in lists.

How do they work?

Clauses

A semi-colon is used to show the close relationship between two main clauses. It is not as 'final' as a full stop. It makes the point to the reader that the clauses are closely related in subject matter. The clauses it separates must be of equal importance and both be main clauses.

semi-colon used to separate two linked main clauses, both about the tram

When I got to the tram stop it was already full of people; I had almost missed the tram for the second morning in a row!

Jake's nan and her pet snake, Matilda, lived close by; Singer Street was only a two-minute walk away from Edmoth Close.

semi-colon used to separate two linked main clauses, both about distance between family members

In these examples, the clauses make sense on their own. There could be a full stop between them, but they are closely linked in their subject matter, so a semi-colon helpfully shows their link.

Lists

A semi-colon is used to separate items in a list when the list requires clearer division between items; for example, if the items are long and detailed, semi-colons should be used.

Chenyl had a great holiday: on Monday, she swam in the sea; on Tuesday, she went shopping at the local market; on Wednesday, she visited the local historical sites; Thursday and Friday were spent by the pool; on Saturday, she enjoyed the water park and on Sunday she packed.

semi-colons used to the separate items in a list

Activity 1

Add semi-colons in the correct places in the sentences below.

a) She checked her bag before she left to make sure she had everything: her bus pass and train ticket all the tools she needed for work her mobile phone and her house keys.

b) The Shans liked the flat on Connell Avenue the best their house had already been sold but the buyers were being difficult.

c) Charlie's bike screeched to a halt in front of the ice sculpture there were people watching so he was careful not to do anything yet.

d) Bobby had a choice of cars: the white car with a new sound system the cute pink soft-top mini or the brand new black four-wheel drive with white leather seats.

/4

Activity 2

Add a semi-colon and then write a main clause to complete the following sentences. (Remember the clause must make sense as a sentence in its own right and should be of equal importance to the first clause. It might provide a contrast or it might be very closely linked to the first clause. You could think of this as a pair of scales which need to balance.)

a) My library card was out of date ....

b) He was the most experienced player ....

c) Doughnuts are one of my favourite foods ....

d) They had nothing to lose ....

e) The weather was perfect ....

/5

Activity 3

Rewrite the following sentences, moving or adding semi-colons if necessary.

a) I didn't do well in Science last year I failed French; my English result was another story!

b) They sailed the seven seas; they climbed the highest; mountains and they crossed vast deserts.

c) The ghost wailed as he wandered the streets the witch soared into the sky on her broomstick; the monsters loomed out of the dark alleyways: it was a strange and spooky night.

d) Both boys enjoyed the funfair however, they thought the beach was better.

e) You can choose from: trifle with; jelly and custard; chocolate profiteroles; with ice cream fresh fruit salad and cream.

/5

8 Colons

What are colons?

A colon is used to signal the introduction of further information. It is found at the start of a list and sometimes between clauses.

How do they work?

Between clauses

A colon can be used between two main clauses where the second main clause explains or expands upon the first main clause.

I felt the snow start to fall upon on my hair: it immediately started to go frizzy!

The witch had a wart on her nose: it was green and poisonous.

Lists

A colon can be used to introduce a list.

I packed my bag this morning: a wooden spoon, a ruler, a potato and some marbles.

In our team we had: Harry, Henry, Huila, Henrietta and Hailey.

Introducing a quotation

A colon can be used to introduce a quotation.

Dr Jekyll begins to change in his behaviour and appearance: 'Dr Jekyll grew pale to the very lips and there came a blackness to his eye.'

In 'War Photographer', the poem starts by emphasising how much the man longs for solitude after being constantly surrounded by the devastating effects of war: 'In his dark room he is finally alone.'

Using a dash instead of a colon

A dash can be used instead of a colon to separate the information at the end of a sentence. It is less formal than a colon, and can make the final piece of information sound much more dramatic.

I felt the snow start to fall on my hair: it immediately started to go frizzy!

Betty could see the ship powering across the waves and she was excited: he was coming home.

Betty could see the ship powering across the waves and she was excited – he was coming home.

Activity 1

Tick the box next to the sentences where the colon has been used correctly.

The sand oozed between her feet: this was paradise.	
Fabian spotted the masked figure walking towards him: a car drove past as he waited to cross the road.	
The island of Hawaii: is in the North Pacific Ocean.	
Our team huddled together: it was our last chance to win.	
The Natural History Museum was packed: with busy people.	
Rosa sat quietly in the tree: listening to everyone.	

/6

Activity 2

Decide whether the statements below are true or false:

a) Colons can show the end of a sentence. True / False

b) A colon can introduce a quotation. True / False

c) Always use a capital letter after a colon. True / False

d) A colon separates two main clauses which contrast with each other. True / False

e) A colon can introduce an explanation or an example. True / False

/5

Activity 3

Add a colon and then write a clause to complete the following sentences.

a) Olwen needed several items at the supermarket ....

b) I quote my best friend ....

c) The world is a strange place ....

d) Kit had all the gear for cycling ....

e) I phoned all my friends that night ....

f) I was all alone ....

/6

Semi-colons and colons in context

An extract from *H is for Hawk* by Helen Macdonald

In this extract from a non-fiction text published in 2014, the writer recounts her search for goshawks in Cambridgeshire.

I knew it would be hard. Goshawks *are* hard. Have you ever seen a hawk catch a bird in your back garden? I've not, but I know it's happened. I've found evidence. Out on the patio flagstones, sometimes, tiny fragments: a little, insect-like songbird leg, with a foot clenched tight where the sinews have pulled it; or – even more
5 gruesomely – a **disarticulated** beak, a house sparrow beak top, or bottom, a little **conical** beak of blushed **gunmetal**, slightly **translucent**, with a few faint **maxillary** feathers adhering to it. But maybe you have: maybe you've glanced out of the window and seen there on the lawn, a bloody great hawk murdering a pigeon, or a blackbird, or a magpie … I've had people rush up to me in the supermarket,
10 or the library and say, eyes huge, *I saw a hawk catch a bird in my back garden this morning!* And I'm just about to open my mouth and say, *Sparrowhawk!* And they say, 'I looked in the bird book. It was a goshawk.' But it never is; the books don't work. When it's fighting a pigeon on your lawn a hawk becomes much larger than life, and bird-book illustrations never match the memory. Here's the sparrowhawk. It's
15 grey, with a black and white barred front, yellow eyes and long tail. Next to it is the goshawk. This one is also grey, with a black and white barred front, yellow eyes and a long tail. You think, Hmm. You read the description. Sparrowhawk: twelve to sixteen inches long. Goshawk: nineteen to twenty-four inches. There. It was huge. It must be a goshawk. They look identical. Goshawks are bigger, that's all. Just bigger.

disarticulated separated
conical cone-shaped
gunmetal grey and dull
translucent see-through
maxillary attached to the jaw

Activity 1 Understanding the text

a) What type of bird is the author looking for?

---

b) What two clues might you have that a hawk has been in your garden?

---

c) What bird is the goshawk often confused with?

---

d) What three features do the sparrowhawk and the goshawk share?

Activity 2 Exploring the writer's technique

a) Why has the writer placed a colon after the phrase 'tiny fragments' in line 3?

---

b) Why has the writer used a semi-colon in line 4?

---

c) i. Explain why the writer has used colons in the following sentences:

'Sparrowhawk: twelve to sixteen inches long. Goshawk: nineteen to twenty-four inches.'

---

ii. Why might you find colons used frequently in reference books?

Activity 3 Try it yourself

On a separate piece of paper, write two entries for a celebrity-spotting book. They should each be a paragraph.

Include information about:

- what makes the person a celebrity
- what they do on a daily basis
- what they look like
- where they live
- what they eat
- other celebrities they might be connected to and how.

Remember to use colons and semi-colons to make your writing clear. Use them to introduce lists and to separate information where appropriate.

Tip

Remember to leave a space after a colon.

1 Plural nouns

What are plural nouns?

A singular noun indicates that there is one person, place or thing. A plural noun indicates that there is more than one person, place or thing.

Singular	Plural
girl	girls
box	boxes
knife	knives

Key terms

consonant these letters are consonants: b c d f g h j k l m n p q r s t v w x y z

vowel these letters are vowels: a, e, i, o u

Most nouns can be singular or plural. This means they are 'countable' nouns. A non-countable noun is one that does not have a plural, for example, 'courage' or 'music'.

The following table shows the most common rules for changing a singular noun into a plural noun.

Singular noun	What to add	Example
Most nouns	Add –s	hair > hairs
Ending in 's', 'sh', 'ch', 'x' or 'z'	Add –es	church > churches
Ending in a consonant followed by 'o'	Add –s or –es (you need to learn these as there is no rule!)	tomato > tomatoes
Ending in a vowel followed by 'o'	Add –s	ratio > ratios
Ending in a **consonant** followed by 'y'	Change the –y to an –i and add –es	fairy > fairies
Ending in a **vowel** followed by 'y'	Add –s	donkey > donkeys
Ending in 'f' or 'fe'	Add –ves or –s (you need to learn these as there is no rule!)	leaf > leaves scarf > scarves
Ending in 'is'	Remove the –is and replace with –es	analysis > analyses

As with all spelling rules, there are exceptions. Some plural nouns require you to alter the spelling more radically. You will need to learn those.

man > men
woman > women
child > children
mouse > mice
person > people
tooth > teeth

Activity 1

Circle the correct spelling of the plural noun.

a) The babys / babies cried when the doctor entered the room.

b) Mr Tran gave each of his classes / class's a surprise test at the end of term.

c) There were too many solos / soloes in the Bollywood dance competition.

d) Those girls took their lunches / lunchs onto the ship's deck.

e) Daria checked the sheep / sheeps had enough water for the night.

f) My sister secretly met her friends / friendes at the ticket office.

g) Yesterday, the childs / children hid when the bell went for lessons.

h) There were no activities / activitys to keep us occupied so we were bored all holiday.

/8

Activity 2

Write the plural of the following nouns next to them.

a) pencil ....

b) bottle ....

c) roof ....

d) axis ....

e) crisis ....

f) phone ....

g) bench ....

h) human ....

i) man ....

j) potato ....

/10

Activity 3

Decide which of the following spellings is correct and circle it.

a)	wolves	wolfs
b)	taxies	taxis
c)	matches	matchs
d)	stimuluses	stimuli
e)	echoes	echos
f)	teeth	tooths
g)	loaves	loafs
h)	crisises	crises
i)	quizzes	quizs
j)	halves	halfs

/10

2 Prefixes

What are prefixes?

A prefix is a group of letters that you can add to the start of a root or base word to change its meaning and create a new word.

en + courage = encourage   dis + approve = disapprove

The following are common prefixes.

Prefix	Meaning	Examples
a–, an–	without	atypical, amoral
anti–	against	antifreeze, anticlimax
auto–	self	autocorrect, autobiography
com–, con–	with	compromise, convert
en–	put into	ensure, enable
ex–	out, outside of	exchange, export
inter–	between	interact, interchangeable
over–	excessively	overrated, overexcited
pre–	before, forward	preschool, preview
re–	again	recycle, rewind
sub–	under	submarine, substandard
super–	above, beyond	superhero, superstar
trans–	across	transfusion, transatlantic

Some prefixes are used to make the opposite meaning to the root word.

Prefix	Meaning	Examples
de–	opposite, reduce, remove	decode, decrease, debug
dis–	not	disinterested, disengaged,
dis–	opposite of	disapprove, disembark
il–, im–, in–, ir–	not, without	impatient, irregular, indirect, illegal
mis–	wrong	misuse, misunderstand
un–	not	unclear, unsafe, unreliable

Activity 1

Add the correct prefix below to the root word to make the meaning of the sentence clear.

il	dis	en	pre	un	de

a) Mia Mars was _____appointed that her scene was cut from the film.

b) It is _____legal to drive a car without a licence.

c) I bought my stepdaughter a ____paid railcard for her train journey.

d) Jensen was _____decided about whether to go to the protest or not.

e) The fishermen were _____raged when their boats were vandalised with graffiti.

f) We _____flated the bouncy castle after Assid's 70th birthday party.

g) The children _____wrapped their surprise presents when they came in from the garden.

/7

Activity 2

Sort the following words into the boxes below to match them to the correct prefix.

act	probable	personal	patient	equal	likely	human
active	qualify	approval	involved	credit	significant	

im	dis	en

un	in

/13

3 Common suffixes

What are suffixes?

A suffix is a group of letters that you can add to the end of a word to create a new word or to change the grammatical purpose of the word; for example, it can change a verb to an adjective.

The following are common suffixes.

Suffix	Meaning	Word created	Example
–ly	characteristic of	Changes an adjective to an adverb	quiet > quiet**ly**
–ness	state of	Changes an adjective to a noun	ill > ill**ness**
–en	made of	Changes a noun to an adjective	wood > wood**en**
–ful	full of	Changes a noun to an adjective	peace > peace**ful**
–less	without	Changes a noun to an adjective	heart > heart**less**
–able	capable of being	Changes a verb to an adjective	read > read**able**

Activity 1

Add the correct suffix below to the root word to make the meaning of the sentence clear.

ly ness ful less able en

a) I felt use ________ when the motorbike leaked and I couldn't fix it.

b) Selena was care ________ not to spill her magic potion.

c) As the storm clouds gathered, a dark _______ fell over the town.

d) Her hair was long and gold ______.

e) She was carrying an arm _____ of books.

f) Ravi moved quick ____ towards the exit.

g) The quality of his work was accept ______.

h) The business was account ______ for its poor sales figures.

i) Hearing the steps moving closer, I became fear _______ of the dark alleyway.

/9

4 Adding –ed suffixes to verbs

1 The suffix **–ed** can be added to the infinitive form of a verb to make the past tense.

walk > walk**ed** dress > dress**ed**

2 If the infinitive is one syllable or the stress is at the end and ends in a single consonant letter preceded by a single vowel, you double the final consonant before you add **–ed**.

stop > stop**ped** hop > hop**ped**

3 If the infinitive ends in a silent 'e', replace the 'e' with **–ed**.

hope > hop**ed** care > car**ed**

4 If the infinitive ends in 'c', add 'k' before adding **–ed**.

picnic > picnic**ked** mimic > mimic**ked**

There are some irregular verbs that do not add **–ed** to form the past tense, but that change in other ways. These need to be learned.

Activity 1

Rewrite the following infinitives in the past tense.

Infinitive	Past tense
cook	
drop	
watch	
race	
shower	
panic	

/6

Find out more

You can find out more about irregular verbs on page 81.

5 Adding –ing suffixes to verbs

1 When the suffix **–ing** is added to the infinitive form of a verb, it forms the present participle. This shows that something is happening now and is continuing to happen.

walk > walk**ing** dress > dress**ing**

2 If the infinitive is one syllable, or the stress is at the end, and ends in a single consonant letter preceded by a single vowel, you double the final consonant before you add **–ing**.

stop > stop**ping** hop > hop**ping**

3 If the infinitive ends in a silent 'e', replace the 'e' with **–ing**.

hope > hop**ing** care > car**ing**

4 If the infinitive ends in 'c', add 'k' before adding **–ing**.

picnic > picnic**king** mimic > mimic**king**

5 If the infinitive ends in 'ee', 'ye' or 'oe' do not drop the final 'e' before adding **–ing**.

free > free**ing** dye > dye**ing**

Find out more

See pages 22–23 for more about the present progressive tense.

Activity 1

Underline the correct spelling of these verbs in the present participle.

a) sleep	sleeping	sleping	slept
b) sit	siting	sitting	siiting
c) create	created	creating	creaeted
d) like	likeing	likng	liking

/4

6 Irregular verbs

Some irregular verbs form the past tense in different ways. These need to be learned.

Some of the most common irregular verbs can be found in the table below.

Infinitive	Simple past	Past participle
be	was/were	been
choose	chose	chosen
eat	ate	eaten
fall	fell	fallen
grow	grew	grown
hide	hid	hidden
know	knew	known
read	read	read
ride	rode	ridden
see	saw	seen
show	showed	shown
write	wrote	written

See pages 20–21 for more about the past tense.

Activity 1

Chose the correct verb from the table above for each sentence.

a) The prisoner __________ another letter to his sister.

b) Try as she might she couldn't help but __________ in love with him.

c) DC Chandry ________ the suspect his rights as he arrested him.

d) I ___________ the money under the rotting tree as arranged with my contact.

e) Rhonda ________ the grey van racing towards her.

f) The two boys had _________ waiting underneath the bridge for an hour.

/6

7 'i before e'

If a word contains a long vowel sound (that sounds like 'ee') and there is not a 'c' before that sound then the spelling rule is 'i before e'.

brief relieve

There are exceptions to this rule (for example, b**ei**ng and prot**ei**n), which you need to learn or check in a dictionary if you are unsure.

Activity 1

Tick the correct spellings of the words below and put a cross next to each incorrect spelling. Correct the incorrect spellings.

Word	Tick or cross	Correct spelling
shreik		
percieve		
species		
beleive		
thief		

/5

Activity 2

In the following sentences, underline the correctly spelled version of the word.

a) I kept the receipt / reciept just in case I wanted to return the parachute.

b) Eva was happy to share her last piece / peice of advice.

c) The carrier bag provided her with a sheild / shield from the rain.

d) To his releif / relief, the interrogation was delayed until tomorrow.

e) Windrow Farm had a field / feild by the river.

f) My friend / freind asked me over to film his latest vlog.

g) Dimitri's little brother has pictures of trucks stuck on his bedroom ceiling / cieling.

h) Their niece / neice stayed over on Saturday night.

i) The cat was feirce / fierce, because it was caged.

/9

8 Silent ‘e’

Some words end in an ‘e’ that is not pronounced. We call this a ‘silent e’. In some cases the ‘e’ changes the way the other letters are pronounced; in some cases it does not.

1 The silent ‘e’ changes the vowel sound before it to a long sound (for example, ‘a’ is pronounced as ‘ay’).

date   kite

Here are some other helpful tips to remind you when to add a silent ‘e’ to the end of a word. English words do not end in ‘v’ or ‘u’.

wave   true

2 Silent ‘e’ makes ‘c’ and ‘g’ soft in a word.

spice   plunge

A silent ‘e’ after an ‘s’ at the end of a word helps to show that the word is not plural.

dense   tease   lapse

(which would otherwise look like dens, teas, and laps)

3 The silent ‘e’ elongates the ‘th’ sound, /th/, as in ‘teethe’ and ‘bathe’.

Activity 1

Underline the words in the following sentences which use a silent ‘e’.

a) In the world of ballet it is essential to have grace.

b) The actor gave his all on stage.

c) The kite careered to the ground in a state of collapse.

d) The smoke disappeared up the chimney flue.

e) During meditation, it is important to control how you breathe.

f) Please take care on the staircase.

/12

9 Commonly confused words

The following words are commonly confused. Sometimes it is because of the way they are pronounced. For example, 'of' is sometimes mistaken for 'have'.

Word	Explanation	Example
did	This is the past tense of the verb 'do'. If an event has occurred in the past then use 'did'.	I **did** my homework.
done	This is the past participle of 'do' and is used in conjunction with 'have/has/had'. It is used to say something happened in the past but that the action has importance in the present.	I **have done** my homework.
was	This is the past tense of the verb 'to be'. 'Was' is used in the first-person singular 'I' and the third-person singular 'he, she, it'.	She **was** talking to my friend.
were	This is the past tense of the verb 'to be'. 'Were' is used in the second-person singular and plural 'you' and first-and third-person plural 'we, they'.	We **were** talking to our friends.
have	'Could' is a modal verb that works with the verb 'have'. When contracted, it is always 'could've'. It is never 'could of'.	John **could** have asked me first.

Activity 1

Underline the correct word needed in the following sentences.

a) I could not believe that he done / did it!
b) We was / were so excited about getting our new royal python.
c) Mrs Brown should have / of let her parrot out of his cage more often.
d) The cafe was / were busy at lunchtimes.
e) Kira done / did her homework after she finished her dinner.
f) She would of / have gone to the party but no one asked her.
g) St Albion's cricket captain was / were so excited to make it to the playoffs.
h) Alijah's horse was / were kept at the local stable.
i) Rosa could of / have answered Han's call but she was angry with him.

/9

Glossary

acronym a word formed by the initial letters of a phrase and pronounced as a word, e.g. NASA stands for the National Aeronautics and Space Administration

adjective a word that describes a person, place or object (nouns and pronouns)

adjective phrase a group of words that acts as an adjective and has an adjective as its headword

adverb a word that gives more detail about a verb, an adjective or another adverb

adverbs of frequency adverbs that say how often something happens, e.g. sometimes or rarely

adverbs of time adverbs that say when something is taking place, e.g. *tomorrow* or *later*

adverb phrase a group of words that acts as an adverb and has an adverb as its headword

apostrophe for contraction an apostrophe to show that some letters are missing when two words are combined and shortened (contracted), e.g. *don't* or *we're*

apostrophe for possession (or possessive apostrophe) an apostrophe that shows that one thing belongs to another thing or person, e.g. the boy's shoes

auxiliary verb a helping verb that comes before the main verb to help express a tense

capital letter an upper case letter, e.g. A, B or C. Lower case letters are smaller, e.g. a, b or c

clause a group of words that work together as a unit with a verb as its headword

colon a punctuation mark : that can be used to introduce a list, examples or explanations

comma a punctuation mark , used to separate information. It can separate items in a list, clauses or direct speech from information about the speaker

common noun a noun that names a general thing rather than a particular one, e.g. *girl* or *car*

comparative adjective an adjective that compares two things, e.g. she is *happier* than him

complex sentence a sentence that contains one main clause and at least one subordinate clause. The clauses are joined together by subordinating conjunctions. A complex sentence is a type of multi-clause sentence.

compound sentence a sentence that is made up of two or more clauses that are equally important and joined together by a coordinating conjunction. A compound sentence is a type of multi-clause sentence.

conjunction (or connective) a linking word that joins words, phrases or clauses, e.g. *if, but* or *and*

consonant these letters are consonants: b c d f g h j k l m n p q r s t v w x y z

coordinating conjunction a conjunction that joins two parts of a sentence that are of equal weight (they are both full clauses), e.g. *and*, *yet* or *for*

determiner a word that comes before a noun and gives more information about it, such as which one it is, how many there are, where it is and whose it is, e.g. an, that or some

dialogue spoken words between two or more people

direct speech the exact words that someone says. Direct speech uses speech marks (or inverted commas) to mark the beginning and end of the words spoken.

exclamation a sentence that expresses emotion such as surprise, enthusiasm or horror

exclamation mark a punctuation mark ! that is usually placed at the end of a sentence to indicate that the sentence is an exclamation

full stop a punctuation mark . used to indicate the end of a sentence, or to show that a word has been shortened or abbreviated

future tense a tense used to describe things that will happen in the future

headword the most important word in a phrase

infinitive the root, or base form, of a verb. Often has 'to' in front of it e.g. 'to play'

inverted commas (or speech marks) a punctuation mark that goes at the beginning " and end " of spoken words

irregular verb a verb that changes in a unique way, not following the usual pattern and often changing the root of the word

list a number of items recorded one after the other

lower case letters smaller letters, e.g. a, b or c.

main clause a clause that contains a subject and verb, and makes sense on its own

main verb the main verb details the main action, state or feeling

multi-clause sentence a sentence made up of more than one clause, each with its own verb; they can include two main clauses, or one main clause and one subordinate clause

noun a word used to name a person, place, idea or thing

noun phrase a group of words that acts as a noun and has a noun as its headword

object the object in a sentence is the person, animal or thing that is on the receiving end of the action (having something done to it)

paragraph a sentence or group of sentences on one idea that forms a distinct section in a piece of writing

past tense a tense used to describe things that have already happened

personal pronoun a word that can be used instead of a noun that refers to a person, people or things, e.g. she, it, his

phrase a group of words that form a unit; most phrases do not have a verb so they are not full sentences

plural more than one. It is the opposite of singular, which means just one

plural noun a noun that is more than one. Most plural nouns are made by adding –s or –es to the singular noun, e.g. foxes or hats

possessive pronoun a pronoun that refers to things that are owned, e.g. mine, yours or his prefix a group of letters placed in front of a root word to add to or change its meaning, e.g. un– or dis–

present tense a tense used to describe things that are happening now

pronoun a word that can be used instead of a noun

proper noun a noun that names a particular person, place or thing, e.g. London, the Queen

punctuation the marks, such as full stop or comma, used in writing to separate sentences and their parts, and to make meaning clear

question a sentence that asks something

question mark a punctuation mark ? that is usually placed at the end of a sentence to indicate that the sentence is a question

regular verb a verb that follows a set pattern, adding different endings, but leaving the root of the word unchanged

rhetorical question a question asked without expecting an answer. It is often used to make an important point e.g. 'Are you kidding me?'

semi-colon a punctuation mark ; that links together two main clauses that are of equal importance but that suggest a contrast or are closely related

sentence a group of words that expresses a complete idea. Sentences usually have a verb and form a statement, question, command or exclamation

single-clause (or simple sentence) a sentence comprised of one main clause. They are also known as single-clause sentences

subject the person, animal or thing in a sentence that is doing or being the verb

subordinate clause a clause that adds information to a main clause but can't work as a sentence on its own

subordinating conjunction a word of phrase that joins a less important part of a sentence (subordinate clause) to the most important part of the sentence (main clause), e.g. 'because', 'until', 'whereas'

suffix a group of letters that can be added to the end of the root form of a word, e.g *–ed* or *–ing*

superlative adjective an adjective that compares more than two things, e.g. she is happier than him, but the cat is *happiest* of all

tense the three main verb tenses are past tense, present tense and future; they explain whether something is happening now, has already happened or will happen in the future

upper case letters (or capital letters) larger letters, e.g. A, B or C. Lower case letters are smaller, e.g. a, b or c

verb a word that identifies actions, thoughts, feelings or a state of being

verb tense the three main verb tenses are past tense, present tense and future tense; they explain whether something is happening now, has already happened, or will happen in the future

vowel these letters are vowels: a, e, i, o u

OXFORD
UNIVERSITY PRESS

Great Clarendon Street, Oxford, OX2 6DP, United Kingdom

Oxford University Press is a department of the University of Oxford. It furthers the University's objective of excellence in research, scholarship, and education by publishing worldwide. Oxford is a registered trade mark of Oxford University Press in the UK and in certain other countries

First published in 2019

British Library Cataloguing in Publication Data

Data available

ISBN 978-019-842159-7

10 9 8 7 6 5

Printed by CPI Group (UK) Ltd, Croydon CR0 4YY

Acknowledgements

The authors and publisher are grateful for permission to include extracts from the following copyright material:

Rachel Joyce: *Perfect* (Doubleday, 2013), copyright © Rachel Joyce 2013, reprinted by permission of The Random House Group Ltd.

Helen Macdonald: *Hawk* (Vintage, 2014), copyright © Helen Macdonald 2014, reprinted by permission of The Random House Group Ltd.

Yann Martel: *Life of Pi* (Canongate, 2016), copyright © Yann Martel 2001, reprinted by permission of the publishers, Canongate Books Ltd.

Jeanette Winterson: *Oranges are Not the Only Fruit* (Vintage, 1991), copyright © Jeanette Winterson 1985, reprinted by permission of The Random House Group Ltd.

Tim Winton: *Cloud Street* (Picador, 2015), copyright © Tim Winton 1992, reprinted by permission of David Higham Associates.

The author and publisher are grateful for permission to reprint the following copyright images:

Cover: MyImages - Micha/Shutterstock. **p15**: Angela Schmidt/ Shutterstock; **p19**: Skinstorm/Shutterstock.

Illustrations by Oxford University Press

We have made every effort to trace and contact all copyright holders before publication. If notified, the publisher will rectify any errors or omissions at the earliest opportunity.